SURF'S UP IN IN PURGATORY

By Michael Spawn

Edited by Michael Spawn & David Travis Bland

ISBN 9781072759638

INVENTORY

III. WHERE PRAYER SALTS THE AIR

IV. COMMUNION PLATTERS

V. CONFESSIONS FOR THE ROAD

FOREWORD

I FIRST KNEW MICHAEL SPAWN AS THE DRUMMER OF Shallow Palace, an unabashed alternative rock band in Columbia with omnivorous, shapeshifting tendencies. Amid all their forays into indie rock, blues, punk and glam, the only consistent feature seemed to be the assured insistence of heavy thunder delivered in just the right places by the intense rock 'n' roller that sat behind the drumkit.

First encountering his writing though, was a surprise of a different sort. Many musicians fancy themselves natural critics, and they are to a certain point, with their sustained interest in the intricacies of a great chord progression or the construction of a proper bridge. At the same time, though, that intense focus can predispose some to be a bit too self-interested and myopic when it comes to taking the wide-angle lens and carefully placing the music in its proper cultural and social context, or with drawing aesthetic distinctions that makes most music legible to most audiences.

This has never been a real problem for Michael. Although his approach is undeniably idiosyncratic, you'll find in these pages a thoroughly inquisitive attitude towards not just music and how we talk and think about it, but how it makes us feel loneliness, friendship, and all of the other porous emotional borders that music seeps through in our lives.

I loved his style and panache from the start, first reading his work in the *Free Times* before recruiting him to the *Jasper Magazine* fold back in 2013. His imaginative approach was a fresh change of pace from the more staid and conservative traps that so many critics and journalists can fall into. Michael was never going to deliver you anything in the standard, pro-forma mold – his approach was to almost constantly take risks, to never be anything less than himself. I'll never forget when he turned in his story on Mark Rapp for *Jasper*, where, amid the standard biographical work and a sharply-observed bit of live music review, he devoted a few hundred words to examine how the jazz trumpeter ate his sandwich.

Those kind of left-field creative tactics make him a consistently great read on so many of the classic rock icons which also populate these pages – from making the case for the Pixies as the true demonic band of the '80s to slyly reinvigorating seemingly played-out debates about Fleetwood Mac and the Eagles, he presents himself as a gracefully awkward inquisitor, operating with a kind of Hunter S. Thompson shiftiness paired with a heart of gold.

Reading these individual pieces all together in a single compendium paints this picture in even more compelling terms, but there's also more here. Michael wisely pairs that work with bits of short stories and creative non-fiction, including a diaristic middle section of vignettes that examine everything from low-budget touring to late-night Five Points reveries, and that too is revelatory. It's not difficult to trace the hard-nosed romanticism of his musical life in the early 2000s to the bold and big-hearted way he approaches writing about other musicians years later. There's a touch of familiarity that is always there, never overwhelming the subject (unless the subject matter warrants it, like his "It Might Get Meta" essay on local music criticism), but nonetheless providing an aura of co-conspirator as much as observer. His work on Dear Blanca, Jake Garrett of Mason Jar Menagerie, and Ryan Sheffield all bear this out in loving ways.

In the end, the best part of this book is how closely it mimics what it's actually like to hang out with Michael, the sharp raconteur at the bar whose opinionated, conversational style would be pompous if not so full of joy and wit, humility and charm. He's the kind of guy you seek out at the party, the one who delivers those surprising takes that you start to warm to after that second beer, which glow with crystal clarity in the humid darkness of a Southern twilight turning to night.

You want to talk with him about anything and everything (but mostly music), with the certainty that you will eventually feel your own humanity brightened.

Godspeed, friend.

-Kyle Peterson
Editor, *Jasper*
June, 2019

For Mary, Queen of the Universe

PART I

EXALTED HEATHENS & UNDERSUNG PROPHETS

The New Oasis

"WE'RE JUST TRYING TO TALK OUR OWN language," Man Man lead singer and pianist Honus Honus tells me, "but most people don't want to hear it. We try to write pop songs but clearly I have no concept of what real pop is." Given that there's no pop convention Man Man won't joyfully mangle, the last statement is almost certainly bullshit. Honus knows how pop music is done, he just avoids it after getting close enough to the mark that no one can say he didn't try and then carries on as though he bears some painful handicap. But it's his career and therefore his call.

What Man Man actually plays is a little difficult to categorize. They gain plenty of favorable (and accurate) comparisons to Frank Zappa and Captain Beefheart, but that's mostly because of the band's interest in idiosyncratic instruments and Honus's gruff vocal delivery. There's also something Vaudevillian about Man Man. Their live show includes horns (brass and bicycle), falsettos coming at you from all cardinal directions, and a wonderfully spastic drummer playing as if each tom-tom is loaded with bomb parts and every night is the last hurrah. In a different era, most any given Man Man song could be used to announce the arrival of a traveling circus or medicine show. All five members (Honus Honus, Pow Pow, Critter Crat, Sergei Sogay, and Chang Wang) wear solid white from top to bottom and war paint on their faces. There is also no downtime to be found at a Man Man show. The music is constant from the beginning on through the end with improvised jams connecting one song to the next. The stage is littered with gadgets, toys, and anything else the band decides might come in handy, making each venue reminiscent of a day care center where the kids grew up but never left.

Man Man is a self-described 'underground band,' but Honus insists he has larger aspirations. "I don't really hear our songs getting played on the radio like Justin Timberlake," he says. "But they should be. I just can't think of anyone else out there who sounds like us…I don't think we're strange. People think we're strange. We're just trying to write our version of what we consider pop songs." He claims to want mainstream success – or at least feels it's owed to him – but is resistant to any of the conventional paths to achieve it. When asked if Man Man would ever sign to a major label if given the opportunity, he doesn't hesitate, though his reasoning is curious. "No. I don't think a major label would ever want to sign us. If they did, the only reason would be to just shut us down. I just can't see a major label wanting to mess around with Man Man." As of this writing, Man Man has a record deal with a subsidiary of longtime punk bastion Epitaph Records.

He may not be too interested in the commercialization that often attends working with a big-name label, but he actually seems optimistic about the current state of independent rock and pop. "The interesting thing about music right now, and it's really great," he says, "is that bands like Modest Mouse, the Shins, the Arcade Fire, and Iron and Wine – you know, diverse styles. But they're charting. People actually care and they're looking for music. It's great that that can happen. It's great that a band like Modest Mouse that busted their hump for fifteen years to be where they're at can be successful. People have the same access to the band as they do to shit like Mudvayne."

There's a lot of contradictions in just these few lines about what pop music is and isn't, making it unclear whether Honus has an all-around distaste for major labels, which would be odd given his enthusiasm for what so many of his contemporaries have accomplished under the auspices of labels that presumably want nothing more than to 'shut his band down', whatever that's supposed to mean, or if he's covering up career instincts that could prove problematic for him in the future. In all likelihood, he's been giving so many interviews every day for so long that he's just stopped putting too much thought into what he says.

At present, Man Man is content to continue roaming the country with their singular, utterly bizarre brand of gypsy rock. But Honus has his own take on what Man Man brings to the table. "Man Man's sound is like water," he says. "Like water in the desert when you've been in the heat for days." If this is his honest assessment, it's a new one, clearly a test run, but I can't blame him for trying out a new response to what must be for him a common question. And for his sake I hope he's right. We should all be lucky enough to become whatever we say we are.

-October, 2008

Finding Emo

LIKE THE GAMING SYSTEM FOR WHICH THEY'RE named, the Ataris are a product of a bygone era. But unlike the Atari 2600 or its sister systems, the band hasn't yet slipped into relic status and probably won't anytime soon. Not enough time has passed and their fanbase, while nowhere near what it once was, hasn't died out. But for many fans, this one included, the Ataris' glory days feel like half a lifetime ago (for some of us, they actually were) and most nostalgic emotions for the band are wrapped up in its work from 1997 to 2003. One might safely assume the Ataris would be fine with this, as they have always been fueled by the dual pistons of nostalgia and emotion.

Despite their perpetual melodiousness and guileless approach to hooks, the Ataris – formed in 1995 in Anderson, Indiana – were always best described as a punk band. The odd ballad notwithstanding, the songs were usually fast and crunchy, and frontman Kris Roe sang with a loud, bratty rasp indicative of too many basement shows and bad PA systems. Still, there was one description the band was never quite able to shake – the dreaded 'emo' label.

Few musical subgenres have been as exhaustively debated and excavated and, by contrast, avoided and maligned as emo.

The word itself is shorthand for 'emotional' and almost never used as a compliment. But in order to connect with a listener, emotion seems like it would be a key factor for any artist. Radiohead are emotional. Refused are excessively emotional. But no one who wanted to be taken seriously would ever categorize these bands as emo.

In his 2003 book *Nothing Feels Good: Punk Rock, Teenagers, and Emo,* then-*SPIN* magazine editor Andy Greenwald writes, "The word has survived and flourished in three decades, two millenniums, and two Bush administrations ... It's been a source of pride, a target of derision, a mark of confusion, and a sign of the times." According to Darren Walters, co-owner of early indie rock fortress Jade Tree Records, emo was "originally a genre of hardcore punk that was less focused on politics and heavy music and more on personal politics and melody."

Both of these assessments are pretty tough to argue with, but the definition I most prefer is my own, where emo refers to punk-indebted rock music characterized by adolescent lyrical solipsism that presents as outward romantic longing. By this metric, the Ataris can be considered emo Jedi masters, because for all the skate punk tempos and snotty vocalization, Roe's lyrics were defined by a near-singular obsession with heartache and unrequited romance, all delivered with an earnestness that can only come from the belief that one's feelings are unique, maybe even unprecedented. If copyright infringement wasn't an issue, any given Ataris record could easily be called *Girls, Girls, Girls.* Instead, we've got titles like *Blue Skies, Broken Hearts....Next 12 Exits* and *So Long, Astoria,* the latter containing the band's only actual hit, a cover of Don Henley's "Boys of Summer," a song that was already pining for the past when Henley recorded it in 1984.

Things changed with the Ataris' 2007 record *Welcome the Night*. This and all subsequent releases tossed aside the band's trademark sound and themes in favor of darker, more intricate musicianship and 'mature' subject matter. The results felt forced. Gone was the youthful urgency that served as the connective tissue between artist and audience. Instead of growing up alongside one another, both factions simply grew apart.

-December, 2016

Psychobilly Sermon

THIS TOUR STARTED IN ABOUT 1986," SAYS JIM HEATH. Despite the fact that he's spent the majority of his adult life on the road, he sounds every inch the born-and-bred Texan that he is. He speaks slowly, but not necessarily deliberately, in a thick molasses drawl. His sentences are broken up by extended pauses, indicating either a scattered mental process, distractible attention, a general lack of interest in the conversation, or some combination of the three. "It's a hectic lifestyle, but we're really lucky that we're able to do this for a living, so I don't complain too much about it."

Indeed, Heath, 58, like many Southern men of his generation, doesn't seem easily given over to complaint. But he's not a chipper fellow, either. Rather, he speaks with the straightforward manner of a man who has long since come to terms with who he is and what that entails. In Heath's case, it means he is the Reverend Horton Heat. And so he will front the band that bears his name, just as he has since it formed in Dallas in 1985.

The Reverend Horton Heat plays a frenetic, blood-pressure-raising amalgamation of punk and rockabilly commonly known as psychobilly, a genre of which the RHH is often considered an early forerunner, at least on this side of the

Atlantic. Within the confines of the RHH's sonic world, the bass is played slap, the drums gallop like Seabiscuit, and the guitar work is relentless and often technically stellar – all keeping pace while the Rev snarls like an amped-up Elvis. These characteristics don't put the RHH at odds with genre standards, even if Heath himself is somewhat ambivalent toward the psychobilly label. "We had the song 'Psychobilly Freakout,' so we kind of got put into that scene," he says. "But I've never really considered us to be a psychobilly band. We do some stuff that probably could be considered psychobilly and we've played a lot of psychobilly festivals over in Europe, so I can see why people would want to put us into that scene."

Psychobilly or not (answer: psychobilly), the Reverend Horton Heat occupies a peculiar place in our culture's musical topography. They're by no means huge stars, but it would be incorrect to call them an underground band. They've never been a major radio presence but anyone who has ever played *Tony Hawk's Pro Skater 3* or *Guitar Hero II* has heard their music at least once. If you purchased a Mazda Miata in the late '90s or early '00s, you may have been inspired by the RHH's "Big Red Rocket of Love," which appeared in all television ads for the vehicle in 1999. The group's fanbase is modest in size but committed, sometimes abrasively so. When I was 17, I was once forced to sit in anxious, blinking silence on a friend's living room couch while a TV repairman held forth for no less than six minutes about why the Reverend Horton Heat was the greatest thing to happen to rock music in decades – possibly ever – and who could not fathom how my ostensibly pro-rock friend and I had never heard of them.

But no matter how many video game soundtracks or car commercials it graces, the Reverend Horton Heat is and has always been a niche band and anyone who has delved into its catalogue even casually can understand why. In character, execution, and style, almost every song is borderline indistinguishable from the next. I realize that "it all sounds the same" is the laziest form of cop-out criticism, but in this case it's almost literally true in a way that makes AC/DC and the Ramones seem like genre-bending enigmas. But this stubborn consistency ultimately works to the group's advantage. If you sort of like one RHH album, it's safe to assume you'll sort of like them all. If you played *Guitar Hero II* and thought "Psychobilly Freakout" hung the rock 'n' roll moon, you'll likely feel the same about "Baby I'm Drunk."

Even the Reverend, with his plainspoken candor, acknowledges this sonic uniformity. "It's a style that's unique to us. We have our own sound," he posits. "I don't think it'd be very good to veer off from that too much ... I've discovered that if we do something that I think is very different from our normal sound, it still sounds like us. It's like we couldn't even change it if we tried."

-March, 2017

The Loneliest Corner in Winslow, Arizona

J UST AS A BASKETBALL FAN CAN'T IGNORE THE LEGACY of Michael Jordan, appreciating classic rock means eventually contending with the Eagles. Their music is ubiquitous in a way that feels borderline oppressive, with songs like "Peaceful Easy Feeling" and "Hotel California" hardwired into the memory bank of anyone who has ever ventured into public or been within earshot of a working radio. This passive-aggressive omnipresence, coupled with their status as the best-selling band in the history of American music, can make even the most well-meaning critique of the Eagles feel about as useful as a critical analysis of carbon dioxide.

But maybe it's time to stand back and see the Eagles for what they really are – not a band as much as a mega-successful cultural entity whose commercial dominance came as no surprise to anyone, least of all the Eagles themselves. Every smash single and sold-out concert carried a whiff of the inevitable, as though Don Henley and Glenn Frey had reached some arrangement with the universe, then settled into untold wealth as the scheme went off like a game of Mousetrap. But even the best laid plans can be thrown askew by circumstance and timing, and the Eagles learned something vital the hard way. While royalty checks can prove an artist's ability to move units, they have nothing to do with moving a legacy in the artist's favor, and there's nothing Irving Azoff can do about it.

Because I was not yet a person, I can't say with certainty how much flak the Eagles caught during their '70s heyday when they were writing big hit records and jetting around the globe, but I'd be willing to go all in and say that they were nowhere near the music lovers' punching bag they are today. Considering they arguably haven't been a relevant act since their brief 1994 comeback, that's a little strange. Why didn't it happen to Fleetwood Mac, perhaps their only rival for the title of Biggest Band of the '70s? Maybe it's because Fleetwood Mac has *Tusk* under its belt while the Eagles never took a single musical risk. Or maybe it's because, while the members of Fleetwood Mac were fucking one another, the Eagles seemed to delight in fucking one another over.

It's a shame that the only dead Eagle is the easiest not to love. Glenn Frey passed away in 2016 and has since been replaced by his son Deacon and country musician Vince Gill, but death hasn't softened his reputation. All of his bandmates, including the ones he never fired, have more or less characterized him as a micro-managing bully who, like all perfectionists, was impossible to please. His songwriting partner and co-head Eagle Don Henley has aged into an unabashed curmudgeon who can't seem to believe how ungrateful we are for the bounty he's bestowed. Musical talent aside, the rest of the guys are pretty much non-entities, with the exception of Joe Walsh. Walsh is the only Eagle generally beloved by all, as well as the only Eagle with a sense of humor. This is not a coincidence.

If there's still any confusion as to why Frey makes such a satisfying target, go to YouTube and watch the band's 1998 induction into the Rock & Roll Hall of Fame, where he offers a master class on behaving like a perfect jackass in public. After standing off to the side, visibly impatient while his bandmates offer their acceptance speeches, Frey takes to the podium. "Obviously, what's going on tonight is a lot bigger than any of the individuals onstage," he begins, before launching into a diatribe against the public's fixation on the infighting and drama that led to the band's breakup (twice), and of which he was usually the cause. This goes on for a few minutes but the whole induction is so bizarre that I could watch an hour of it. Frey concludes with his thesis, which just so happened to be the title of the band's most recent single: "Get over it," he intones with practiced gravitas.

The same man that once instructed the world to take it easy now needs us to just get over it. These may seem at first like kindred expressions, but their differences are striking. One is kindly, practical wisdom and the other has no one but the speaker's interests at heart. It seemed important to Frey that people like me get over whatever 'it' is, but I just wasn't made for such an ambiguous task.

-April, 2018

Nostalgia, Inc.

I T'S CLEAR BY NOW THAT COLUMBIA DIGS ITS ROCK nostalgia. Take last month's Peter Frampton and Steve Miller Band concert at the Colonial Life Arena. By most any measure, it was a good show. My dad is a big Steve Miller fan from way back, so I got tickets for his birthday. The entire night was a hitfest, one after another, all performed for a crowded house that needed no winning over. But with the exception of Frampton's excellent instrumental version of Soundgarden's "Black Hole Sun" and some road-tested jams that could have seemed improvised if that's what you needed to believe, the concert contained few surprises. Miller's performance felt especially perfunctory, flawless in the way a machine is flawless when it only performs exactly one function and never overexerts itself.

This isn't a problem, really. A bunch of people paid money to hear songs they already knew and loved, the musicians performed them without incident, and everyone went home happy. Nobody could argue that this concert wasn't a success. But it was also pure, undiluted nostalgia and there wasn't a soul on the stage or in the audience who bothered pretending otherwise. Don't mistake this observation for cynicism. Nostalgia can be healthy. Nobody stays nineteen forever and real devotion to a band or artist doesn't disappear just because you've got a 401K and own the lawn you mow, so if Steve Miller is coming to town and you want to be relive a time when you were a midnight-toking space cowboy yourself, I see mostly upsides. Mostly.

Next week's Def Leppard and Journey concert, also at the Colonial Life Arena, looks to be an interesting if slightly uneven bill that exemplifies the nostalgia industry's willingness to throw together the biggest names possible and write off any incongruity as just the cost of doing business. And these bands *were* big. On the strength of 1983's diamond-selling album *Pyromania*, it could be argued that Def Leppard was patient zero for the pop metal that came to define commercial rock for the rest of that decade. But Journey will be the main event.

It's tough to overstate how gargantuan this band was in its prime. Not only was it a relentless hit machine between the late-'70s and late-'80s, but it boasted one of the most gifted rock vocalists to ever draw breath, the now-retired Steve Perry. But Journey's greatest contribution to the world will forever be 1981's "Don't Stop Believin'," a power ballad of near-ridiculous grandiosity and the world heavyweight champion of karaoke songs.

These arena-ready legacy packages can be lots of fun and are in no way sinister in and of themselves, but their pervasiveness highlights an unfortunate reality for rock fans, especially those coming of age right now – the days of rock 'n' roll as a major cultural force are finished. Genres that were once relegated to the margins (hip-hop most of all) now lord over the pop landscape, their position secured after being absorbed by youth culture, the ultimate swing vote and primary source of any music's ruling status. The natural result is once-dominant rock acts teaming up to ensure maximum financial returns. Def Leppard and Journey, two bands whose paths would never have crossed during their glory days now pooling their remaining cultural cachet in order to pack arenas, fit into this model as if it's the most natural thing in the world. And given the current climate for rock bands, it might as well be.

This is the new normal. As the curtains close on the rock era, count on more and more legacy acts blowing into town to sell your own memories back to you, gently used.

-August, 2018

Gravity Rides Again

INDIE ROCK HAS ALWAYS BEEN AN AMORPHORMOUS descriptor, but when pressed to define it in specific terms – as a recognizable genre rather than a given artist's lack of reliance on major label resources – no band came closer to hitting the mark than Modest Mouse.

Like so many things, this could just be a matter of timing. Upon my first exposure to Modest Mouse as a junior in high school, I sensed right away that something was slightly askew. Until that point, my reactions to music were purely visceral. I either liked something or I didn't, and little thought was involved. But I had no idea what to make of Modest Mouse. "What's going on here?" I probably wondered. "Where are the choruses? What kind of singing voice is this supposed to be? How old is this person?" And most importantly, "Do I like this?" The band clearly hadn't considered me at all when writing these songs and so I was forced to make a decision. Should I stay or should I go? And so, Modest Mouse became the first band I liked on purpose.

This came with unexpected responsibilities and I knew right away I was on turf not to be tread lightly. Modest Mouse fans tended to be a serious lot whose devotion was often a core part of their identity. As is commonly the case with underground

bands, these fans treated Modest Mouse as though it were some
juicy secret shared only by those high-minded enough to
appreciate the trio's subtle, wicked genius. But the spell was
broken when the band's 2004 album *Good News for People Who
Love Bad News* became a genuine smash thanks to its lead single
"Float On," which dropped like an atom bomb on rock and pop
radio. Bewildered as fans were in the immediate aftermath, no
one seemed less sure about how to proceed than frontman Isaac
Brock.

From his grown-man lisp to his open infatuation with
drugs and alcohol, Brock has always been one of indie rock's
more intriguing characters. As a songwriter and guitarist, he
can't be called anything but a true original. Since forming
Modest Mouse in 1992 with drummer Jeremiah Green and
bassist Eric Judy, Brock has built a body of work defined by the
absence of definition and this unpredictability is a large part of
the allure. Any given Modest Mouse song can be an exercise in
manic energy or it can be stubbornly mellow. It can be disarming
in its beauty and elegance and then dive headlong into
morbidity. Subject matter is a crapshoot – hope, loneliness,
revenge, Orange Juliuses (Juliei?), plane crashes, Charles
Bukowski, wild dogs, rats, cockroaches, pretty sunsets, teeth, god,
shoeshine, what people are made of (nothing but water and shit,
it turns out), and long drives with nothing to think about have all
been given their due. Brock's guitar work can come across as
deliberately amateurish, a quality that's difficult to square with
his evident grasp of economy and open space. Even in moments
of chaos there was always a sense that he had things firmly under
control.

"Float On" was the moment when the tide shifted and
Brock suddenly seemed ill-prepared for the reality of one of his

creations heading off into the world on its own. This isn't to say that he didn't intend for "Float On" to be a popular track. With its jubilant guitars and relentless disco beat, the song is one long hook, catchy in a way that's anything but accidental. But he wasn't ready for anything he'd written to be *that* big, and it showed. What was once a trio is now a seven-piece band, as if Brock had no better idea as to how to spend all that money than hiring more people to stand on stage with him. With such a large ensemble and Eric Judy's departure in 2011, it's no surprise that Modest Mouse's post-*Good News* work shifted. 2007's *We Were Dead Before the Ship Even Sank* and 2015's *Strangers to Ourselves* aren't bad albums if you take them on their own, but within the larger context of Modest Mouse's career, Brock sounds exhausted with his own peculiar brand of musical parlor tricks. It's almost as if thinks he has cracked the code to a good Modest Mouse song and is now loathe to stray too far from the formula.

For nearly a decade, Modest Mouse helped define the indie rock genre by never fully defining itself. Still, there is always the chance that Brock will right the ship. Until that day comes, I'll live with my decision and float right on.

-October, 2018

If This is the Mac, the Mac is Back

POP MUSIC LORE IS RIFE WITH TALES OF RECKLESS drug use, rampant sex, and explosive egos. The list of bands that can claim all three is so long that it's kind of boring. But only one took them to the highest possible degree, turning the sort of dysfunction that would end lesser bands into its second-biggest strength. That band is, of course, Fleetwood Mac.

The Mac is currently on a world tour, as it is wont to do in those rare moments when its members can get on the same page about anything. But this tour is different. Guitarist Lindsey Buckingham, one of the band's major songwriting forces and lead vocalists, was fired from the band in April of last year. Any Mac tour raises questions about who will show and who's got better things to do, but among the band's classic lineup, a *firing* is pretty much unheard of, especially with Buckingham on the barrel's end.

Fleetwood Mac began as an English blues band in 1967 that saw a slew of players come and go, with the only constants being drummer Mick Fleetwood and bassist John McVie (hence the name). This period produced plenty of good music and a few minor hits, but it wasn't until the ever-prescient Fleetwood met American singer-songwriter Lindsey Buckingham in 1974 that he saw a real opportunity for his band to become more than just a respectable niche ensemble. Buckingham joined the ranks, bringing along his musical and romantic partner Stevie Nicks, and the classic Fleetwood Mac was solidified: Fleetwood, the McVies (John and his then-wife, singer-keyboardist Christine), Buckingham, and Nicks. The first album recorded with this lineup, 1975's *Fleetwood Mac,* may have caused blues purists to despair, as so many things do, but the general public liked what it heard and the LP ushered a handful of songs into the pop canon. While not an immediate smash, *Fleetwood Mac* eventually became the second-best-selling album of 1976, bested only by a live record by some rogue guitarist from Humble Pie.

The pressure to record a worthy follow-up was high, but the band, quite high itself, more than delivered with 1977's *Rumours,* an album so steeped in cocaine and drama and sex and lyrical passive-aggression that its mythology might have stolen the spotlight had the music within not been so damn good. The band's hot streak continued with the brilliantly idiosyncratic double album *Tusk* in 1979. Hit-and-miss records followed, but this opening trinity represents the best of Fleetwood Mac. There were more makeups and breakups, both personal and professional, until the band officially reunited at the behest of the new U.S. president-elect, one Bill Clinton. A Big Mac fan as well as a big Mac fan, Clinton had made "Don't Stop" the musical cornerstone of his campaign, so it came as little surprise when he asked the band to perform it at his presidential gala. Any remaining bad blood was set aside and Fleetwood Mac performed for the benefit of a nation in which only two of its members could legally vote, spurring a wildly successful full-scale reunion tour.

* * * * *

Given the opportunity, most any band would claim that each member is essential to the whole. Fleetwood Mac has never, to my knowledge, made such a claim. The irony is that their case, it's actually true. For at least two generations of fans, these five people *are* Fleetwood Mac and one missing ingredient threatens to ruin the recipe. But Buckingham is a unique case. Though he has often been cast as, and admitted to being, the band's control-obsessed, pigheaded problem child, he is also the only one of the five who might be possessed by something resembling genius. He always cared the most except when he didn't care at all. If Fleetwood Mac were the American government, Fleetwood would be its pragmatic president, McVie his quietly easygoing vice, and the rest of the band congress, with Buckingham as Senate majority leader. And as long as the administration remained popular with the voters (that would be us) President Fleetwood was content to let his most powerful senator make the important calls. Until now, that is.

The official line on Buckingham's sacking is that he couldn't get on board with a rehearsal schedule. This second-hand news sounds suspicious at first, but considering Buckingham's general temperament it's not beyond possibility – though the 2017 release of *Lindsey Buckingham/Christine McVie*, which featured every member of Fleetwood Mac but Nicks, puts a damper on the 'too-busy-Lindsey' defense. In any event, Senator Buckingham is out. Replacing him on the globe-spanning tour are Neil Finn of Crowded House and Mike Campbell, head Heartbreaker to the late Tom Petty. Both top-tier musicians to be sure, but it says a lot that it takes two guys of such talent to replace one Lindsey Buckingham.

* * * * *

...And now that he's gone, which of the remaining rulers will emerge? Among rulers, there are but bad lovers, as Goody Nicks once so elegantly claimed in song. All are bad, but only one can call himself in good faith the Mac caravan's worst lover. At this point in the journey, a few of the roadies and load-in crew who like to keep an eye on the book the bookmaker is making are already letting shadowed whispers float like duckling feathers from their lips, desert-dry to a pair. But even if you catch one of these feathery whispers, could you understand that which it said? Perhaps. Perhaps not. But if you hear it right and plain you now know with a certainty that causes the point spread to genuflect and the inside tip to curse itself for not coming to you first that the smart money is on...Finn. He is the least-known commodity on the caravan and as such is well positioned to become whatever his companions need him to become. Maybe even whatever you *need him to become. Indeed, there is excitement in a fresh face but Campbell has that, too. What's more, Campbell has something Sir Finney does not. Campbell has a problem. His broken heart is a problem, but we shouldn't speak of death these weeks. Campbell has a problem that few have spoken of aloud in deference to his talent and kindly temperament. Campbell may make disappointing love from Greece to Sweden and then paint Paris a light nauseating gray, but a ruler he simply is not. Does Campbell know this about his own character? He must. He is not a ruler but nor is he a common fool. He has never risen from second-in-command and now the chance is lost to the cruel downwinds of time. His ruler, the one called Tom, he of the Gainesville Pettys, had fallen for good. If Goody Nicks had grown cold toward her ancient incantation then it would be he, Finn told himself, who would prove that rulers have since time immemorial made bad lovers and a mere shift in the ruling ranks can not undo what Goody Nicks once sang. And dare she dream her immortal decree*

over, he will find the tallest grass and demonstrate his lackluster form. And all will be well as the Caravan rolls on…

* * * * *

The tour seems to be proceeding without incident, but we'll see for ourselves when the band comes to Columbia Friday night. Until then, the rumors will have to do.

-February, 2019

Nearsighted Pilgrim

ON PAPER, A PIXIES/WEEZER SHOW CIRCA 2019 looks to be a dicey affair, with ample opportunity for the whole thing to crumble under the weight of nostalgia's dark side. The business of being in a touring rock band is perilous enough for the young, never mind two groups whose debut records appeared in 1987 and 1994, respectively. Some things can only disappoint.

Fortunately, this double bill at the Colonial Life Arena did not. After a tight set by English rockers Basement, whose singer Andrew Fisher sounds not unlike a Suffolk-bred Rivers Cuomo, the Pixies meandered onto the stage to rapturous cheers. Frontman Black Francis, who even as a young man didn't fit the traditional mold of the 'cool rock singer,' stared out into the ocean of people through what appeared to be some quality sunglasses. "Who does this guy think he is?" I wondered to my girlfriend, but she didn't know either. Once the light show started, though, the answer was obvious. Francis wasn't trying to look cool, though he kind of did. The shades were entirely practical, as it's unthinkable that the Pixies completed their set without sending at least one concertgoer into an epileptic seizure. Yes, light shows are usually a good idea.

This was my second time seeing the band and both times I was left feeling that the Pixies were wholly uninterested in whether or not I or anyone else enjoyed the evening. It's humbling in a way to see a band not speak a single word of greeting or thanks, never once ask its enormous audience, "How ya feeling out there, Columbia?!" or some such thing. Nor did their performance betray any evidence that the Pixies themselves were having a good time. They played their set with zero mucking around and no effort at all to seduce the audience into loving them, as if we didn't already. One is forced to admit that the Pixies are either alarmingly confident in their music or they genuinely don't care if people enjoy the show. I suppose both are possible. Either way, it made me want to shake all four by the shoulders and remind them how cool their job is and that it's OK to have a little fun up there. But what do I know? Maybe it was the best night of their lives.

Weezer boss Rivers Cuomo was far less inscrutable, which is pretty weird considering he's usually about as easy to read as Tolstoy. But due to the surprise success of Weezer's cover of the 1981 Toto hit "Africa," his band is experiencing a resurgence in popularity he likely had written off long ago. So, with his milking gloves on, Cuomo seemed bent on enjoying every moment. For a man approaching 50, he's remarkably agile, running this way and that across the stage, delivering plenty of his now-familiar white-boy-who-loves-urban-slang patter. It can get a pretty embarrassing and makes one wonder how much self-awareness Cuomo actually possesses. Still, he's got a natural sense for what people come to hear, thereby keeping fan disappointment – no matter how old the fan – to the barest possible minimum. My personal quibble is that Weezer only played one song, "El Scorcho," from its 1996 watershed *Pinkerton*. But there was plenty to keep the grouches like myself happy, even as the band went down a list of its more questionable recent hits, bullet by bullet.

If anything, it was a sobering reminder that the Weezer era that matters most to me doesn't matter most to the band, or at least Cuomo. It would be unfair to demand he stay in the past with me when he's so clearly loving the present. I could spill plenty of ink on Weezer's current trajectory, but we're square for now. They've got my money, I've got their songs.

-March, 2019

PART II

PREY FOR THE SCAVENGERS

The Passenger

"*AND WHAT'S YOUR NAME, BOY?*"
I was standing at the wig counter when the voice came from behind, wielding a reedy twang that cut through the reverb and noise in the cavernous showroom. My travel companions aside, nobody here was any less a stranger to me than any other. But I knew whose voice it was.

Minutes earlier, a somewhat bored-looking middle-aged man and I passed one another in the crowd. We shared a brief glance as passersby often do and his entire demeanor changed in that instant. His eyes lit up with sinister delight. At first, I just assumed that he had mistaken me for somebody else. Still, there was something about his smile that made me not want to show him mine. I made a straight shot for the wig display and didn't look back.

The wigs were arranged before me on disembodied mannequin heads, some with a celebrity's name hand-scribbled on the forehead. There were a few that could have suited the occasion but Charles Nelson Reilly's hair stood out as especially elegant. I took off my cowboy hat and once the piece was snug and secured around my scalp, I turned around. I had intended to give the man a fake name – probably Charles – but seeing that smile at close range threw my presence of mind. "My name is Michael," I said.

Before I could ask him his name, he snorted and said, "I don't think so. Your name is Sheila."

"Sheila?" I said. "No, you've got it all wrong. Sheila is my godmother's name. I'm Michael."

"No, sir. You're Sheila now."

I waited for him to explain as he scoured my face for some sign that I understood what he was telling me. Just when the silence began to feel threatening, he patted me on the shoulder and said, "I'm just foolin', buddy. No hard feelings." Then he turned and disappeared into the crowd, just one more face in a galaxy of them. After returning the wig to its head and the cowboy hat to mine, I did the same.

I reunited with my friends outside. The flea market made for a welcome break in the monotony of the road but plenty of driving still lay ahead. So, after pointing the van toward Chicago, we were back to chasing down the miles, one by one.

-Somewhere in Kentucky

* * * * *

He didn't look much older than us, but he spoke with the directness of a man who knows he's already lived his best day. He wore a baggy gray sweatshirt and his hair was military short. Most importantly, he remembered the agreement we'd reached not long before, while the sun was still up. "We're with the Witness Protection Program," I said.

"Just the four of you?" he asked. I nodded and he gave each of us a once-over and shrugged. "A deal's a deal." Knowing he might have to claim later that he hadn't seen four underage young men enter the club, he turned his back to light a cigarette. Taking the cue, Brett, Luke, J, and I slipped into Chicago B.L.U.E.S. When he turned back around, he was alone on the sidewalk.

I bypassed the bar and the band and made my way to the far back, behind the stage. After fighting my way through a gaggle of drunk women, I made it to the bathroom. Inside, I found myself alone for the first time in seventeen hours. I stared at the greasy mirror for a few seconds, making sure I was still who I thought I was, and then took a long sip from the bottle of Canadian Club I was keeping warm in my coat pocket. The reverberation from the bass drum rattled the dank and tiny room. Indeed, drummer Big Ray was a hard-hitter who dominated Chicago B.L.U.E.S.

Once out of the bathroom, I stood at the right of the stage, just inches away from his floor tom. He was fat, black, stoned, and played with a reckless combination of desperation and glee. He glanced at me occasionally, winking one red eye as he slammed away on his drums. By this time, the others had assumed positions within the crowd and I staggered over to join them. I didn't know how to express it at the time but I had never experienced a musical performance so authentic. I almost threw up. We were finally there – here – and I was transfixed. Having only arrived in the city an hour earlier after more than thirteen on the road, I expected, or maybe feared, that I would be too exhausted to let the city eat me alive, but I was wrong.

-Chicago, IL

* * * * *

With our veins saturated in heavy blues and smuggled booze, we
took to the streets. Saturday night in Chicago was in full swing
and we walked through Boys' Town as people went about their
activities. In time, we returned to J's studio apartment so Greg,
Sandra, and Luke could get some sleep, but I wanted more of
whatever was going on outside. J and Brett agreed to join me,
and we left our friends to deal with their dreams.

    We crossed busy streets, moved through trees, all of them
skinny and naked and dancing in the wind, and jumped down
mammoth concrete steps to the rocks at the shore of the inky
black everything that was Lake Michigan. To my left were the
skyscrapers and the lights and the cars, to the right I could only
just make out a pier below a brilliant Ferris wheel. I wanted to
walk to it but knew that my shoes would deteriorate and my feet
would rot clean off if I even tried. Instead, I sipped whiskey with
my friends, stared ahead at the water, and exclaimed over and
over that we were the luckiest sonsofbitches in the world to be
there, seeing what we were seeing, and seeing it together. After a
while, it was time to move on. We crossed back over onto the
sidewalks that bordered Lincoln Park, marveled at Goethe's
statue, and passed through Boys' Town once again on our way
back to J's. I slept easily and with fine memories. Tomorrow was
only a few hours away. I wanted more of the same but didn't
know what I'd done to earn it.

In the morning, we had breakfast to find and a baseball game to
make. The Cubs were continuing their stand against the Pirates,

and to show my support I designed a posterboard advising the
baby bears of Chicago to put some stank on it. I rarely attend big
time sporting events, but caught a whiff of the spirit and cheered
loudly for the hometown boys. I held up my sign between
innings, knowing my parents were watching from back home,
but the television cameras never found their way to us, just below
an empty row of metal seats. We cheered and ate junk and
sipped three-finger hot chocolate. John Cusack conducted the
7th Inning Stretch, after which we snuck down to the field-level
seats to watch the end of the game. I was now sitting next to a
small child who stared at me with big, freakish eyes and seemed
to have a good understanding of what the Cubs needed to take
the game. "Two more runs," he said, "and the Cubs will win."

"I know," I lied. He turned and shrieked toward the field.

As we drove that night, a hard rain began to fall upon the city.
Parking was hard to find but we managed, and then ran through
the downpour to the door of a jazz club called the Green Mill.
We paid the cover charge and strolled inside. Our table was lit
by a single candle, as all the Green Mill's tables were, and our
wet, disheveled appearance stood in contrast to the tucked-in
Polos and white eveningwear of the rest of the patrons. They
were all silent, as they had been instructed to be by the manager,
a portly woman with a terrible, grating laugh and no respect for
her own rules. I was immediately ill-at-ease, feeling of a lower
class than the dead-eyed young professionals that surrounded the
bar and occupied the other tables. The room was dark and quiet,
save for a man in sunglasses tinkering expertly on a Hammond
organ behind the bar. He wore sunglasses and had a broad smile.
I wondered if he was blind.

After a while, Miss Morgan materialized behind the bar to polite applause. She took the microphone, nodded, and went into the first number. Her voice lacked nothing in the way of passion and natural sweetness. She was young and fair-skinned, her hair was up in a bun, and she smiled often as she sang, taking a cue from the legion of lady crooners that had come before her. Her presence shifted the atmosphere from one of cool resignation to something looser and less afraid of whispers. After the first song, she opened the floor up to requests. A bit early for that, I thought, but this is jazz. A world I seldom see. With that in mind, I requested "That's Life," and was pleased when she said she would give it a try even though her admission that she was a tad rusty on the lyrics turned out to be an understatement. She made it no farther than the bridge. But the organ player, I knew, could have played that song all night.

The set was good but I was feeling squirrelly and wanted a change of scenery. My companions felt the same and we gathered our things. As we filed out the door, I turned back and blew Miss Morgan a kiss, which she returned with a smile. I silently wished her luck, knowing that life can be tough when you make your living singing from behind the bar.

-Athens, GA
April, 2011

The Passenger II

THREE DAYS DEEP INTO OUR TRIP AND THIS IS THE first honest chance I've had to put pen to paper and sort out everything that has and hasn't happened so far. Given the current national temperature I thought it would be fitting to sample the food at the Wall Street Deli here in Washington, DC, a city that just might jog itself into the Atlantic and where a clearance level is as common a thing to have as a middle name. I must surely stand out as a tourist as I don't have an ID badge swinging from my neck. It's a curious name for a deli where the all-female staff screams at one another in Spanish and there isn't a single financial periodical to be found on any of its tables or news racks. And they insist on this boorish type of jazz. Not a thread of sensuality coming through the speakers.

The 21st Amendment Bar and Grill is a welcome change. They want six of your dollars for just one of their domestic draft beers, but the music is better and the chairs are easier on the ass. Their televisions are silently reporting on the recent comments made by Susan Sarandon concerning the Pope and his supposed Nazi sympathies. Our nation appears to be in fine working order.

The shows so far have been going well. I had the strange pleasure of meeting Sarah, this airy-eyed girl who claimed to listen to our music all day long at home and then walked thirty minutes to Galaxy Hut to catch the show. How she found the music in the first place was something she had trouble explaining, but I think it was just the booze that had dulled her memory. Before that, on Sunday, we once more visited Harrisonburg, VA and were treated graciously as always by our regular hosts. Even with seven other people in the van, there hasn't been much of the road anxiety I've gotten used to on these tours. It likely won't stay that way, but so far I have precious few complaints.

-Washington, DC

* * * * *

Our Rhode Island hosts are the excessively accommodating Karrie and her adventurous bulldog, Rocko. I took Rocko to the park this morning and we walked past a shimmering pond lined with briars and tall, naked trees. Providence in the Fall feels neutral, crisp and mild, a good reference point for any city that just can't seem to get the season right. Rocko and I both understood and appreciated this as we strolled along the dirt path. There were other dogs and one of them, this tiny black thing with wet marble eyes, came over to say hello. It changed its mind once it got close and saw how much bigger Rocko was and how easily he could have killed and eaten it, but that isn't Rocko's way. He only stood, towering over the little thing and capturing it in the shadow of his pink and white belly, which

caused it to shake in fear. Their encounter was cut short when
the black dog's human leash-holder, whose name remains
unknown, tugged him away and smiled at me as if to say, "Dogs,
brother. Crazy things, huh?" I nodded back. Crazy things.

Rocko led the way to a small cemetery where some people
have been buried for hundreds of years. The stones were
polished, even the really old ones, and the sunshine fell to their
tops and spilled over onto Rocko's paws if he happened to be
sniffing the inscription. Over there was Rose, wife of Michael.
That's all it said. I asked Rocko if he thought Rose would be
satisfied with such a legacy. And who was Michael, anyway?
What was so great about him? Rocko and I shrugged and moved
on.

-Providence, RI

* * * * *

The weather was hot and uncomfortable but I took solace in in
my friends and our lazy conversation. Then came the danger.
We were utterly vulnerable to whatever happened outside, which
started off as this fireball dagger dragging itself across the air but
ended with rain that felt hotter on the top of my head than the
North Carolina sun.

We drank and gambled the afternoon away in Asheville's
Green Man Brewery, but once the rain came and threatened our
plans, we were off, running against water and wind before
climbing inside Greg's van. The eight of us in the back barely
had room to scratch our asses, but we rode on as Greg and Josh

dreamed of Utopia, an American city created entirely according to their shared vision, which they couldn't ever agree upon.

It didn't matter really. First, because they rarely agreed on anything. Second, because the supposed altruism of the would-be sovereign duo, despite their words and the volume at which we all reacted, was just a distraction from the massive bummer that was braying at our ears. It was what had made our borrowed afternoon at the brew shack so pleasant, so vaguely elicit. By the very nature of our excursion, we were, in theory, allowed to do whatever we pleased whenever, save for load-in times and unforeseen traffic problems. But we knew that this night would be our last together and it gave the afternoon the air of a stolen rendezvous, something far off the plan, but perfect, and made more so by the knowledge in the back of our minds that we it was all about to end. After this last beer.

We had been full of hope that morning and couldn't foresee the day ahead being anything less than the monumental send-off we all deserved. Some of us were sore and exhausted from bad sleep, but happy knowing we were together. Our time was coming to a close and I couldn't help but marvel at the ease with which we had all learned to live with each other in such a small pinch of time. Lucas, Josh, and Wil had agreed the night before, over music and beer, that they would get new tattoos. I considered it, but opted out, feeling theirs would be enough.

We left Ryan's apartment and broke up into separate teams for ink and food, convening later at a bookstore where a blonde woman from Brooklyn spoke to a small audience about her recent book on the joys of homemaking. From there it was the brewery where everything coalesced – the feeling of embracing new friendships, immediate trust, wanting to know about one another on a level that was intimate but not intrusive. We were there together and I was happy just to sit back and survey the scene, knowing I was among comrades now, all of them and me, speaking to one another about things we cared about and thought were funny. Lucas hovered over the talk with his camera, hunting for angles and shots, many of which he abandoned without snapping a single photo. Wil and I talked about Dr. Thompson – his work, his life, and the documentary films that attempted to explain both. Brett shared anecdotes from home to anyone who would listen, and an audience wasn't hard to find. Later, Tami and I discussed New Zealand, its culture, the dangerous animals in Australia that I had never seen, and while she talked I couldn't ignore the nagging sense that she was someone I had met before and had known well, with her eyes, the way she did her hair, her style of dress, her Northern brazenness. George hung by quietly, listening to all of us, as he is wont to do in large groups, while Greg strolled from conversation to conversation, telling stories, letting me fill in my favorite parts.

Too soon, the rain picked up and we were forced to call the afternoon. I wanted to stay in the humid shanty drinking beer with my friends and listening to Jane's Addiction play over the stereo system. I wanted to play darts. I wanted to get so wrapped up and involved in every word everyone was saying that it made me tired just to think about it. It was my last chance, and everyone's, to do it and make it count.

We made it back to Ryan's apartment, only to be faced with the dreaded goodbye, that departure that faces you with the reality of the life that awaits back home, if only you could remember how to get there. As I hugged Lucas, Tami, and Wil, I said stupid things like, "I'm glad we made friends," and, "It was fun touring with you guys." They were all true but woefully understated. There was more that I didn't have the time or the energy to say. So we part, and you get in this car and I'll get in that car, and I can't wait to see you again and hell yeah man, we're going to tear it up next time. But nobody knows when the next time will be, if it comes at all. It's the not-knowing that I hated and still do.

-Asheville, NC
May, 2011

Won't You Be My Stranger

SHUFFLING DOWN THE SIDEWALK ON HARDEN STREET, I pass the bar where a handful of people I think I think I know are nestled among tobacco clouds, while others skitter around in white dresses and pink collars, sniffling and shouting profanities through come-hither smiles. We are probably the same on some base level but there might as well be a language barrier preventing us from understanding – much less loving – one another, as if we were all thrown here together during some collegiate overseas exchange program. The whole scene reminds me how close I am to terminal loneliness and how I'd be in much less danger if I could force myself to love what they love and shout at the top my lungs whatever they shout with such ecstasy at the top of theirs. Our greatest shared cultural touchstone, I realize, is Hootie & the Blowfish. Just how we feel about it might be, I think, quite different altogether.

Approaching the back lot of duplex, I light a Pall Mall and try to think about politics or sex or rock 'n' roll – anything, really, to get my mind off what is, all things considered, Columbia's biggest deal. Maybe because of too much whiskey and too little sleep, the cigarette tastes like the poison that it is and I stomp it out.

Once inside, I almost shout for Michael Rouse. I don't know what to make of how weird Five Points has gotten and Rouse's general perspective is pragmatic to the point of being surreal, and often spot-on. The neighborhood has seen an upshoot in beatings and rapes – some only attempted, but only some. A shooting here and there, wolf-at-the-bar pickups, general unease. If there's a positive result to all of this, it's the way the Five Points mainstays have come to depend upon one another for companionship and safety, conversation and all the other whatnot. Everything else is just terrifying. If Scorsese – for whatever insane reason – decided his next subject would be the Five Points of today, he'd do well to ditch the *Let It Bleed* tunes and roll tape with some Creedence. They're the best band for the job at hand. Fogerty can be uplifting and angry and cautionary all in one song, and that's exactly what we need. We need "Susie Q" as we order the drink that will prove fateful. We need "I Wrote a Song for Everyone" to tuck us in at night. But it's late and Rouse prefers keeping the wee hours to himself. I trudge upstairs and, rather than bother him, prepare for some solitude of my own. I begin by flipping through my records. If we're in as much trouble as I suspect, we're going to need some serious music to distract us. I land on Billy Joel's *The Stranger* and drop then needle.

It was on this record that Joel first attempted to shed his "Piano Man" image, which, of course, resulted in failure. But the album itself was a major career boost, and deservedly so. *The Stranger* is a curious pop artifact and a fine collection of songs. Most of all, it's a snapshot of an insecure artist taken the precise moment he goes from success to superstar. It's easily Joel's least self-aware record.

He often come across in the press as a fundamentally lonesome man prone to bouts of self-pity and for whom contentment is always just out of reach. This Joel is not the Joel of *The Stranger*. But, like all great art, *The Stranger* only makes me think about myself. The melodies and lyrics contained within have practically nothing to do with my routine experiences, though I share its creator's essential restlessness.

Now we're on Side B, where Only the Good Die Young. I will never understand why this isn't played at Confirmation parties. I sure didn't hear it at mine.

-July, 2011

Trunkload of Broken Hearts

THE OLD ADAGE ADVISES THOSE TREADING THE creative whirlpool to 'write what you know,' and although Jeremy Ray has never been one to pay much attention to platitudes, he certainly embodies this particular chestnut. Jeremy writes only about that which he has studied, mulled over, chewed up, and swallowed whole. In short, Jeremy writes most often about what he knows best – himself.

This isn't exactly ground-breaking stuff. First-person observations and self-analysis are as common to the songwriting game as majors and minors, but unlike many songwriters, Jeremy's songs are seldom confessional, at least directly. Instead, he rips joyfully through tunes about spiritual uncertainty, gratitude for what he's learned and curiosity about what he hasn't, all with a swaggering sincerity that dares a listener who may have some insight to jump in and share it. As for songs built around big questions about life before and after death, Jeremy doesn't sing as though the lack of an answer keeps him up at night. Sometimes asking the right question is a victory in itself. Even the somber numbers contain these victories, however small. And Jeremy has never been one to keep a victory to himself.

In "Broken Wagon," he sings "I could be wrong, I could be right/ But I'm probably not." Whether he's referring to the former or the latter isn't specified. Maybe Jeremy himself doesn't know for sure. Maybe the answer doesn't matter at all.

I've known Jeremy Ray for nearly a decade now. We've been bandmates, friends, collaborators on numerous projects, and drinking companions (though, somehow, never all at once), and as a result I've witnessed firsthand the evolution of his abilities as a songwriter and a performer. There was a time when Jeremy would insert into his lyrics whatever thought or item crossed his mind or immediate field of vision. He owned lots of denim and worshipped at the altars of Isaac Brock and Joe Strummer. After spending his entire young life rhapsodizing over the spiritual aspects of human existence, he was turning his gaze outward for the first time, all at once celebrating and criticizing the many facets of the adulthood he had only recently entered. Sometimes he would literally write about an item just because it happened to be in the room with him, and that item (guitar strings, for example) would remain permanently in the song, never to be tampered with or second-guessed as long as the composition lived.

His most recent music finds him staggering happily across the seldom-trod middle ground between inward and outward inspection. It's true, the subject he knows best is himself, but like all good writers before him, he understands that the 'self' is not only the matter and mind of the creator. It encompasses all aspects of his understanding – pain and joy, loss and freedom, and the razor-thin line between family and good friends. He gives them all fair treatment, sometimes sounding like a crooner eulogizing his own bygone childhood. But even when he laments, Jeremy never strays from his defining musical mantra: "Leave your broken heart in the car," he once wrote, "we're here to dance."

PREY FOR THE SCAVENGERS 61

Jeremy's shows are always rollicking affairs and whenever he makes his way back to our shared hometown of Greenville, South Carolina, it's an occasions for old friends to gather and drink, dance, sing, and (if you've got the chops, daredevil) sit in with the band on a number or two. Jeremy makes few demands of his audience but he has never been one to quietly abide a lack of intimacy. He wants you right there with him. He's a stubborn-ass Carolina kid raised on punk rock with a great big heart of whiskey and gold. He wants your attention and you'll give it up if you're smart. The lyrical subject matter may be Jeremy Ray himself, but the object of delivery could be any one of us.

-August, 2011

Subterranean Home, Sick Blues

I T'S A TRUTH HELD IN THE MOST SACRED OF REGARD IN certain subterranean sects of modern society that music, much like love, is not something to be experienced passively, but instead is something to be done, and done with such emotional precision and a heart whose rhythms are tuned perfectly to the needs of its owner that it informs every action performed by the lover or, as it might be, the music maker, the singer of the songs whose voice harmonizes effortlessly with the warming winds, floating calmly to the doorsteps of subterranean homes.

I've seen many places like this but none will ever feel more like a home to me than the one that exists in some tucked-away corner of Fountain Inn, South Carolina, where the only lights to shroud the stars come from a convenience store through the trees and a lone streetlight humming quietly over the adjacent road. The liquor store next door has been put to good use. I've had to park my car in front of it on particularly festive nights that attract more than the usual crowd of singers, strummers, and sketchbook Shakespeares, but it stays dark at night and never intrudes on the twinkling tapestry above if anyone should find reason to step outside and breathe cleaner air. The house is brick, but holes here and there dictate that it bow to the whims of the world outside. When the Carolina air is cold, so is the house. If it becomes comfortably warm or blistering hot, so goes the climate of the subterranean home. It's the the sort of house that hosts so many comers and bids goodbye to so many goers that a curious neighbor, if there was one, might puzzle over which of these excitable young people actually live in the brick house by the streetlight and which have just come to visit, drink, have a smoke, and see the show.

In a way, Jake Garrett has a foot in each group. It's true that the affable, twang-spoken guy with long, braided hair is an official resident and the center of its musical goings-on, but he might also be its biggest fan, an incurable admirer of the unsaddled creativity that takes place within the walls of his home. Although primarily a singer and guitarist, Jake is able to produce something worthwhile from nearly any instrument he touches, and one quickly gets the impression that he derives just as much pleasure from his own songwriting as he does watching others work, surprising themselves with what they are able to accomplish in their own playing and writing. And this is the key to Jake's merit as an artist. Although enormously talented himself, he possesses the rare combination of musical patience and human warmth that continuously brings out the best in those who have the good fortune to play with him. Due to his creative attention deficit, it's difficult to keep a solid count of all of the music projects Jake is currently involved in, but his most inspired work at present comes through the alternative country/bluegrass ensemble Blueroots and his most recent endeavor, the blues-rock trio Mason Jar Menagerie.

With regard to the latter, it can safely be said that blues-saturated rock 'n' roll is nothing new. In fact, the genre has experienced a renaissance in recent years, so it isn't much of a coincidence that listeners experiencing Mason Jar Menagerie for the first time usually offer favorable comparisons to the Black Keys and early White Stripes. But while such parallels work as an acceptable reference point, they don't do much to explain how Jake, his sister/drummer Susan Garrett, and bassist Ameer Raja approach their music, because for all of its hoopla about rebellion and youthful aggression, rock 'n' roll is a genre steeped up to its elbows in tradition. Tradition can be mined for all it's worth until the foundation is all that's left, that hard-wired concrete slab on which the mass of imitators stands. Mason Jar Menagerie are not among them.

When placed in the wrong hands, blues-based rock 'n' roll can be an exhausting, lumbering beast that must be tolerated before we are allowed to move on to something that more efficiently steamrolls the human soul. But when it's done properly – that is, experienced moment-to-moment on both ends of the transmission, it reminds a listener how much fun and therapeutic rock 'n' roll can be and why so many of its adherents choose to pick up a guitar or pair of drum sticks in the first place.

Mason Jar Menagerie makes no claims of reinvention. There is no flash, no inane pretenses. There is only Susan, bouncing on her throne, attacking the drums with her whole body, Ameer, laser-focused on nothing but the groove and pushing the train steadily down the line, and Jake, wailing with his mouth and fingers and perfectly willing to play for seven hours straight if you'd let him.

But it isn't necessary.

It isn't necessary because, when the show is over and the lights have gone down, the band and whoever has the good sense to follow them will return underground and the music will continue on long into the night. Drinkables and smokeables get passed around, stories traded like precious artifacts, anthems of the moment created and quickly forgotten. When we're all back, huddled in that subterranean home, we are reminded that music doesn't only exist on the stage or on the record. It blossoms and grows and fills our lungs wherever there are artists willing to share with and nurture one another into realizing talents they didn't even know they possessed. The only thing affecting us will be the many moods of the weather outside as we drift closer to another morning.

-September, 2011

Every Night an Ocean (Every Song a Ship)

AS ANYONE WHOSE HEART CAN FALL TO ACHING FITS OF wanderlust will tell you, the pleasure afforded by a classic American road trip is dependent entirely on the company you keep, your own mental stability, and the music. Some would argue that the music is the *only* thing that matters. And the music that matters most, at least in the early stages of any proper road trip, is the music playing during the moment when you realize you are no longer home. You're seeing more than the usual number of out-of-state plates and exit signs to nowhere towns and the atmosphere in the vehicle is a one of optimism, the sort that can be marshaled only by the young. This moment is brief but you'll know it when it comes. You'll know it because your heart will feel too big for your body to hold. "Died of a heart attack," someone might comment about you later. "The thing just popped right there in his chest. And they were only just past Charlotte." These brief three or four minutes when your heart might theoretically combust are the ones in which your trip has become a Road Trip, and the song of the moment is terribly important. For the eight of us, riding together in the old van, that moment came just as Ryan Sheffield came chirping through the speakers.

The song was "Promises," the third track off of his long-playing *Head for the Coast*, and there couldn't have been a better tune to shake my consciousness awake to all of the possibilities the road to Boston and back had to offer us. Bryan Highhill's brass melody over Sheffield's opening chords sounded like the lackadaisical whistle of a tipsy street-roamer who's resolved to head back to a place where things made sense. Sheffield sings calmly but confidently about his commitment to self-improvement and laments his regressions from that end. It might sound trite to put it in those simple terms, but to hear the song, there can be no mistaking Sheffield's honest dedication to the person he knows he is capable of becoming.

* * * * *

As much as "Promises" was just the right song for my Road Trip moment, it might also be the perfect song to embody the first of two personalities that exist on *Head for the Coast*. The first is a man who speaks plainly of his hopes for the future. Ryan's straightforward, confessional lyrics work best when he lets this aspect of himself take charge, but there is another side of him at work on the record. If the first looks to the future with optimism and determination, the second is just as adept at turning toward the past. For Sheffield, the moments in life that have yet to materialize are experiences to be tackled with your spirit on fire, but the past is different. Unlike his future, Sheffield's past seems to be something he understands perfectly, and that level of understanding brings out longing, self-ridicule, even anger, and can evoke in a listener crippling nostalgia for past experiences – places we've lived, people we've loved and lost touch with, those tiny golden moments we have all spun quickly through and spend the rest of our lives trying to explain to each other and, mostly, ourselves. The bop-pop of "Jasper," the tight-saddled street rock of "One for the East Bay," and the haunting "Bitter City Cold" are all examples of this more trenchant and, at times, troubled side of Sheffield.

* * * * *

The ten tracks on *Head for the Coast* exist only in the forever-ago and tread swiftly toward the blinking beacon at the end of the tunnel, with the exception of one. "A Letter to Brenna Part II" will always live in the moment of its conception, whenever that may have been. Even though love remains the skeleton of all art, it is still, at least at first, disarming to hear a young man stirred so passionately to shed any pretense of irony or distance and make a simple and self-assured declaration of endless devotion to the woman he can't live without. Ryan wrote the song for his then-girlfriend and now-wife Brenna and, listening to it, one marvels at the courage and talent it takes to write something so confessional and peaceful and comforting. Sweating under the burn of Asheville's summer sun, I watched the two of them become husband and wife as Bryan Highhill played an airy, instrumental version of the song. Anyone who was at the wedding will tell you that it was one of those tiny golden moments you hope never to forget. It makes you wonder what Part I is like.

The record exemplifies more than the dual sides of Ryan Sheffield. If you can't immediately bear witness to his lion-hearted live performance, the record stands as a fair-and-square jumping off point to the moods and feelings he can stir up in a listener. His talent is clear from the first listen and he navigates his different songwriting personalities with grace. But if *Head for the Coast* was the honeymoon, then his latest, *The Shadowbox EP*, makes it clear that the honeymoon is over.

On the surface, *The Shadowbox EP* is like the former record's shorter little brother. Sheffield's prior style and subject matter are both present – earnest attempts at reconciling the what-once-was with the come-what-may, references to specific friends and places, and a vague yearning for a perfect world that might come to life if only certain aspects of this one were a little bit different. To only skim the EP's four short songs might leave one with the impression that it's a mere extension of its predecessor. But sit somewhere quietly and listen. Sheffield's measured singing and the sparse instrumentation offer a small, implicit challenge to the listener. There aren't any bombastic horn or guitar melodies, none of the buoyancy that elevates *Head for the Coast*'s more celebratory turns. And so, he is asking you to sit and listen.

In the paranoid bomb shelter of modern music, this is a tall order. Asking someone to settle down and pay attention to a song they've never heard or heard of can be like asking them to wait doe-eyed as you guide them through an exhaustive retelling of the dream you had last night. But, like most labors of discipline and love, it's worth it. And these are the things that Ryan Sheffield doesn't leave home without.

The record opens with "Jeremy Ray's Front Yard," a song that has been in Ryan's live repertoire for more than a little while but assumes an odd sense of dread when committed to tape. The lyrics offer shadowy optimism as he describes the pleasure of listening to the music of his friend and frequent collaborator Jason Waller, as well as the knowledge that, with patience and good company, life always gets better. But there's a sadness in his voice this time around that undercuts the Sheffieldian belief that tomorrow can always be better than today.

"I Don't Know Why" is the EP's most confessional moment. Light and catchy, Ryan describes the aspects of his personality that he tries and somehow always fails to understand, like his inability to look cops in the eye and his nightly dreams about the ocean. *Shadowbox*'s most thoughtful lyrics tentpole the song, "Ivy League Desk." This track is the most like its stepsiblings on *Head for the Coast* in terms of instrumentation and tone, but completely defines the overall pathos of *Shadowbox* when he sings, "Hold your heart like it's some kind of prize and you'll never get it back." "Bird on a Wire" (or, "Leonard Cohen Rained on My Honky Tonk Parade," depending on its author's mood) is another song that has been road-tested to a razor point and efficiently closed the lid on *Shadowbox*. Its lyrics commend his older brother's reliable stoicism and predicts without a scrapling of doubt his twin sister's success as an actress. As for himself, he's just the bird, singing heartily and as best he can, always aware that a livewire cable is a dangerous place to spend the whole of a day or young adult life.

* * * * *

If you demand irony in all things and can only feel comfortable with people and music that will wink and nudge you out of your own hardwired discomfort with yourself, Ryan Sheffield's songs will instill panic. In his music and, more importantly, his relationships with others, Sheffield doesn't use mannequin bravado or protect himself with cleverness and cynicism. It's clear by the end of the first song, live or on record, that this is an individual with determination, basic human decency, and most importantly, all of the talent and more required to make friends out of fans and believers out of friends wherever he goes. I'm grateful for all of his music, but most of all "Promises." Without it to carry us through that first real Road Trip moment and into the big American unknown, I dread to imagine what might have happened out there.

-November, 2011

So Hush-Hush

~Part One: Jersey Devil~

I MET THE DEVIL AT AN O'CHARLEY'S IN NEW JERSEY, JUST outside Newark. I had been driving north since the early morning and began to feel the early stirrings of highway psychosis some time after nightfall. A break from the road and a couple of drinks seemed like the smart play so, after checking into the first motel I came upon, I made my way to the O'Charley's just across the street. It was nearer to closing time than I had expected and the place was dead. A classic rock radio station played at a low volume while a waiter dozed in a corner booth. The restaurant's sole customer was perched on a barstool pouring a raspberry margarita down his gullet. I'd never laid eyes on him before but knew immediately who he was – the devil himself.

My gut impulse was to turn back but some combination of curiosity and pride compelled me forward. With all of the nonchalance I could fake, I moved to the bar and took a seat two stools down from him. To my relief, he didn't acknowledge me. The bartender, a stocky Lebanese fellow of about twenty-nine, ambled over and raised his chin. I ordered a Killian's Irish Red and was just about to take the first pull when the devil, exhaling with deep satisfaction, slammed his empty glass onto the bar. I turned reflexively at the sound and couldn't help staring as he picked salt crystals out of his teeth with the pinkie nail of his left hand, which was about three inches long and more resembled a shark's tooth than any fingernail I'd ever seen. (The devil is left handed, it turns out, and if that tidbit surprises you, I invite you to consider the etymology of the word 'sinister.') This went on for a long half-minute before he felt me gawking at him, at which point he slowly turned his head and stared right back.

Spellbinding and frightening in equal measure, his eyes nearly knocked the wind out of me. They fairly glowed blue and his gaze was bottomless. He was of indeterminable age and cut a towering figure even when sitting down. Instead of the slacks or trousers of your typical O'Charley's hangabout, he was wearing some sort of black leather kilt, which might have seemed feminine were it not for the obscene bulge pointing in my direction. This, along with a pair of steel toe Doc Martens, was all he had on below the waist. North of the pole, he wore a suit jacket over a white collared shirt while a black necktie hung loose around his neck. He had a burn victim's pocked and cratered skin and more teeth than any creature I've ever seen or heard about, each of them black and filed to a sharp point. He had no horns to speak of but there was definitely a tail peeking out of his kilt. It wasn't red or forked but mammalian, not unlike that of an adolescent buffalo. It could safely be said that he'd be hard to miss in a crowd.

Finally, in a robust baritone with slight reverb, he said, "You know who I am, don't you?" I started to say something but my tongue and throat were dead dry, so I only nodded. "We're square then, because I know who you are too, Mikey Boy." As proof, he proceeded to run down some of my particulars, and not just things like my name, date of birth, address, blood type, average annual income, and social security number. He also recounted in vivid detail a certain nightmare older than my memory itself, one of those grotesque picture shows that intrudes upon so many nights for so many years that you eventually just accept it as a fact of your nocturnal inner life, often dormant but never quite finished with you.

I desperately wanted to direct his focus elsewhere. After a swig of beer to wash down the dust I said, "So... do you come to New Jersey often?"

He glowered at me. "Do I come to New Jersey often? "That's the best ya got? Jesus Christ." He snorted and turned away.

This was going poorly.

I tried again. "What, uh, brings you to O'Charley's?"

The bartender appeared with another raspberry margarita. "Cheers, Immad," the devil said, raising the glass. It was empty in less than nine seconds, an achievement he commemorated with a hearty belch. He motioned for another and then, without looking at me, said, "The pepper jack cheese wedges."

I didn't know who he was talking to. "Come again, sir?"

He swiveled his head. *"The pepper jack cheese wedges!* I don't like to repeat myself, ya dig?"

"Uh-huh." I felt my forehead break out in sweat.

"This particular O'Charley's has the best pepper jack cheese wedges east of anywhere. And I've tried'em all. I just went to town on about three pounds of the stuff. Oh, and call me 'sir' one more time you'll be choking on your own teeth."

"Got it. So, what should I call you? You know, socially. Conversationally. Whatever this is."

"What should you call me? What should *you* call *me*?" He threw his head back and belly-laughed, the sound of which was like thunder rolling directly overhead. "*Call me a cab, baby, I'm drunk enough for another go at the archangel!*" he howled. "No, really, seriously though, I'll tell you what to call me." Here, he cleared his throat and assumed a professorial air with a Churchill-esque flourish. "As it happens, I go by many names, some of which you may have heard – Satan, Lucifer, Mephistopheles, El Diablo, His Satanic Majesty, Sick Nick, the Deceiver, the Dark Lord, Mr. Bad Example, the Father of Lies, the Mack Daddy of Misery, Split-Foot, and innumerable others, some in languages no longer spoken by any living tongue. Each has its own charm and you may address me as whichever you please without fear of reprimand. But if you want the full splendor of my attention, you'd do well to address me as Old Scratch. It is, I must admit, my favorite." And then, Churchill no more, he leaned in toward me. "Ya dig?"

"Yes."

"Yes, what?"

"Yes, Old Scratch."

There was that black-toothed smile again. "Good boy, Mikey.

Just then, the opening bars of "I'm Eighteen" by Alice Cooper came piping through the restaurant's sound system. Old Scratch groaned. "Ah, jeez. Not this guy again." He turned his head and spit on the floor.

"Not an Alice Cooper fan, huh?" I asked.

"Damn straight. He's nothin' but a scarecrow with a mascara habit whose biggest hit is about the last day of school.

He's turned my whole crusade into Dr. Seuss on Ice. Guys like him make me look like a friggin' clown."

"Guys like him?"

"Yeah, they know the kids are gonna eat up whatever gets their parents' panties in a bunch so they pull out some phony Prince of Darkness shtick. *And it works!*"

"But everyone knows it's just an act. Nobody actually things Alice Cooper is evil. He wrote a golf book."

"That's the problem! Evil's my business! It's not supposed to be an *act*. It's not supposed to be *fun*. It's not whatshisface running around on stage with prosthetic breasts, for Chrissakes!"

"Marilyn Manson?"

"That's the guy. Sweet Christmas, I've never seen someone put so much effort into pretending to be me. And people love that shit. Look, I know evil music, alright? That ain't it. That's a goddam cartoon." He shook his head in disgust. "Immad! What's the holdup? I'm drying out over here."

I didn't want to get him any more agitated than he already was but my curiosity got the better of me. "What about Dio?" I asked.

"Who, Ronnie? I love Ronnie. Hell of a guy. Not a bad fisherman, either."

"Ozzy?"

"Osbourne's gone soft. He's a good egg for the most part but dropping acid every day for a year and biting heads off bats doesn't make someone *evil*, just weird at parties. You're looking at this all wrong, Mikey Boy. Your little writing gigs have got you thinking you know a thing or two about music but you're focusing on the wrong thing just like everybody else. The headbanger stuff is all fine and dandy but most of it's got nothing to do with me. I don't know how that idea got into everyone's head but I'd like to rip it out, ya know what I mean?"

"So what music *is* evil, then?"

He waved a dismissive hand. "Not much these days, I can tell ya that much. But it's out there."

"Like what?"

Immad appeared with our drinks and Old Scratch guzzled his raspberry margarita in the usual fashion. I waited for an answer but he stayed silent, staring intently at his empty glass. He began tapping his shark's tooth fingernail on the bar top. I could see that his gears were in motion, so I waited. A smile crept across his face and his eyes lit up like torches. "That's it!" he said, pounding a triumphant fist. "I've got it, Mikey Boy!"

"Oh yeah?"

"Oh yeah. The whole mindset out there about evil in rock 'n' roll needs to be straightened out and you're gonna help me do it."

"How?"

"Here's what we're gonna do. I'm gonna lay it out for you. The whole thing. The real deal, ya dig? And then you're gonna write it and get it out there. You're gonna give people the facts and then they won't be fooled by those hackheads and their preschool horror shows anymore."

It didn't exactly strike me as slam dunk idea but I'd be lying if I said I wasn't intrigued. What the hell, I thought, and reached into my pocket. "Alright. I don't have my voice recorder on me but my phone should work fine."

Old Scratch shook his head. "Nope. No recording, pal. There can't be any record of this conversation."

"Then how am I supposed to quote you? If your words aren't in the story, then neither are you."

He leaned forward and put a hand on my shoulder. In an instant there was a pain where he touched me. It felt as if someone was dragging a deodorant stick over a fresh sunburn, so much so that I yelped and nearly fell off my stool. He pulled his hand away and the sensation disappeared. "Oh, sorry, Mikey Boy," he said, not unsympathetically. "I really need to start wearing gloves when I go out. Anyway, listen close. You can't quote me in whatever you write. That's a dead giveaway that we talked in person."

"So?"

"*Sooooo*....I'm not exactly what you would call – how to put this – street legal, if you know what I'm saying." Old Scratch was clearly wasted and I did not, in fact, know what he was saying. With a heavy sigh, he continued. "Look. I used to work for – work *with* a certain someone. We had our differences, yadda yadda yadda, we went our separate ways and long story short, I'm not supposed to wander off the reservation. Ever, for any reason. Now, you know me. I like to take my little excursions here and there, come up for some pepper jack cheese wedges once in a while, maybe throw back a few dozen raspberry margs, no big thing. It's just that this certain someone has eyes and ears all over the goddamn place and if word got around that I was out and about, things would get very, very bad for Old Scratch. So you can't record anything I say, ya dig? And when you write this thing you've gotta do it in a way that doesn't give away that we talked or met at all. Is this making sense, Mikey?"

"Yeah, but how am I going to have any credibility? The information has to come from somewhere."

"Don't worry about that. Just say....Ah-ha! Say I came to you in a dream."

"A dream."

"Bingo."

"I'm skeptical that the whole dream prophecy thing is going to fly, Scratch. But if I write anything having to do with our conversation, I'll keep you out of trouble. I give you my word."

"'Atta boy. Now the world is finally gonna hear my side of things. The world is finally gonna learn where the real evil is in rock 'n' roll, ya dig?"

I didn't bother mentioning that the 'the world' doesn't read my stuff but assured him that I did indeed dig. And so Old Scratch unloaded take after take for the next fifteen minutes. He even told me his favorite band. When it came time to settle up, he patted his kilt and told Immad he must have left his wallet at home. The poor bartender looked ready to cry. I didn't want his night to end like this so I took care of Old Scratch's tab, which was not small. He must have been drinking raspberry margaritas and eating cheese wedges for hours before I showed up.

We went out to the parking lot. Scratch was game to keep talking but I needed some sleep. "It was good to meet you," I said. "You're an interesting guy, Scratch."

"Not many people can say that," he replied, "And yes, I am." He stuck his hand out but I shook my head. "Whoops. Almost forgot. Well, that's that then. You take care now, Mikey Boy. I'm counting on you to do right by me."

"Goodnight, Scratch."

"I know where you sleep."

With that, we broke off in opposite directions, hopefully never to see each other again.

~Part Two: For All the World to Read~

B ack in the mid-eighties, Tipper Gore and a legion of concerned parents were struck with self-righteous fervor and demanded that record companies slap a Parental Advisory sticker on every musical recording they deemed immoral, sacrilegious, or simply too strange to dissolve easily on the tongue of the average consumer. Their basic thesis was that certain music just wasn't made for certain ears and it's tough to argue with a notion so completely void of details. Such vague concern for America's youth won the day for the Parents Music Resource Center, if not in totality then undoubtedly against heavy metal.

It's true, a great deal of American metal was (still is, really) sexist and violent, but no legitimate believer in god could realistically take its penny dreadful interpretation of devil-worship with any seriousness. True followers of the Dark Master of Even Darker Arts aren't concerned with huge riffs and leather pants, pyrotechnics or floor-rattling bass guitars. That's just the show. When the devil wants you, he will get you, and he will do so subtly, with little fanfare. And that's why the devil's favorite band is, and will always be, the Pixies.

Between the incessant howling, the ominous whispers, the meth-panic guitars, and those cuddly little bass lines, the Pixies are the most Satanic band that has ever existed. Frank Black, Kim Deal, Joey Santiago, and Dave Lovering make Slayer seem like schoolyard rascals. No rock band before or since has bathed so gloriously in the River Styx – not even Styx. This might not be evident upon first, second, or even tenth listen, but that's kind of the point, the precise trait god warns makes him so sinister. *"He will come to you with brazen hooks, searing lead guitar, and an increasingly bald head. Trust not, lest ye be thoroughly sliced, like so many eyeballs."* (Spawn 1:66)

The devil takes many forms, but within the idiom of music he has emerged in one band only. While metal bands are content to scream about torrents of blood raining down from the sky or to command listeners to bring their daughters to the slaughter, Boston's demon-pop darlings take a more scenic route on the long and winding road to hellish delirium. If evil was a road trip, most supposedly devilish artists would deliberately hit all the toll roads, if only to ensure that the hapless booth attendant is forced to stare into their soulless eyes. But the Pixies take the country roads that the GPS doesn't recommend. There is more damage to be done on those underdriven dirt roads. The terrain is less populated and therefore feels safer to the average hitchhiker, thumbing his way to a pot of fading ember at the end of Satan's rainbow.

Take a song like "Dead," the most Luciferic track off rock's most wicked record, *Doolittle.* It's the perfect expression of everything the Pixies and devil-rock stand for. The unspoken rule of most rock and pop has always been this: A song's refrain should be dressed as payoff and redeem anything lacking in the verse prior. "Dead" takes this to its pinnacle. The verses are chaotic and strange, at once repellent and hypnotic. The guitar line is completely unpredictable and always a hair offbeat. Frank mutters, then he puppy-yelps, and sometimes he seems to be barely talking. And then, just when you've accepted the reality that you aren't listening to a pop song by any normal pop artist, here comes the refrain: a joyful, debauched, surf's-up-in-Purgatory guitar line that features no lyrics and yet makes you wonder why any guitar player with at least four working digits never came up with it before.

There are other examples. On "La La Love You," drummer Dave Lovering delivers his lead vocals with Bundy-esque charm. "Here Comes Your Man" is the ultimate threat. And in "Monkey Gone to Heaven," when Black yowls, "God is seven," one can't help but picture him standing triumphant against an ever-darkening and lightning-ridden sky, fists raised while the Almighty bleeds at his feet.

They say god works in mysterious ways, and that may be true, but Satan loves what he does so much that he likely hasn't worked a day in his life. The devil holds the universe's greatest temptations and while murderous, diabolical heavy metal has its appeal, it shines nothing like the apple hanging delicately from the tree, promising everything and looking so damn good doing it. That's evil. And that's the Pixies.

-July, 2015

Two-Hand Tapping

A WEEK OR SO AGO, D. T. BLAND AND I WERE SITTING in a local tavern, drinking Yuengling, talking literature. Next on his hit list, he said, was Truman Capote's true crime opus, *In Cold Blood*. "It's a great book," I told him. "You'll like the writing, I think. Capote's got an interesting style."

"How so?" he asked. "I've never read him."

A tough question, to be sure. After a pause and a swig, I decided to appeal to our shared misfortune of having grown up as music geeks and library junkies. "Truman Capote is the Eddie Van Halen of the written word," I said at last, assuming that settled it the matter.

D. T. stared at me. "Go on."

I leaned back in my chair, winding up for the time-honored barstool pastime of nonsense theorizing. "Alright," I said. "Eddie's an amazing guitarist, right? A virtuoso. The sounds he gets out of the guitar can be achieved only by him."

"I think I'm with you so far."

"Well, Capote's the same way. He's a demon on the typewriter. Where Eddie's licks demonstrate a manic obsession with the possibilities of his chosen medium, Capote's stuff could only have been written by someone who has dedicated his life to the narrative purity of serious prose and the pursuit of the perfect sentence."

D. T. nodded slowly and ran a finger around the rim of his glass. "But there's a but."

"There is a but," I said. "The but is – that's as deep as it goes. Both Van Halen and Capote embody what can be accomplished when your best trick is performance alone. For all of their talent, it's just a show. It's 'look-what-I-can-do.' With one major exception, there's an emptiness at the heart of what they do. A deficiency of soul."

He seemed unconvinced. "I'll just read the book, I guess."

Conversation moved on to other things, but questions began to gnaw at me. *Did this notion have any legs? Was it too simplistic? Too inside? Or could this template be used to explain the relationships between other word- and axe-slingers?* I had my doubts but couldn't ignore the possibilities of such an endeavor. So what follows, offered in the spirit of civic responsibility, is a brief rundown of five renowned authors and their guitar hero counterparts. The list is by no means complete but it's a good start at cracking the shell surrounding perhaps one of the greatest non-mysteries of our time: Can our literary tastes explain our musical leanings and vice versa? (Note: *The previously mentioned exception to the Capote-Van Halen hypothesis is provided below.*)

Ernest Hemingway = Johnny Ramone: This one should be fairly obvious. Ramone is a paragon of six-string efficiency. No excess, no fluff, no showing off. Likewise, Hemingway made it nearly impossible for anyone to write in lean, declarative sentences without betraying his influence. Johnny viewed lead licks and solos the same way Hemingway viewed subordinate clauses – as frivolities to be deployed only in the most desperate moments – i.e., to communicate climactic prosaic intensity or when Phil Spector is waving a revolver in your face.

See: *In Our Time* by Ernest Hemingway
      Rocket to Russia by the Ramones

Kurt Vonnegut = Joe Walsh: By 1975, the Eagles had finally accepted what everyone else knew all along: They were flamboyantly incapable of rocking. Enter Joe Walsh, an insatiable party monster who brought a sense of mayhem to a band that saw his self-destructive behavior as a means toward something no amount of money could buy – rock 'n' roll credibility. Like Walsh, Kurt Vonnegut took his fun seriously. This attitude was key, allowing both men to produce work that not only jibed with their drunk-uncle-at-the-reunion personas, but offered golden nuggets of humanist wisdom via lines whose goofiness directly correlated to their profundity. Walsh did for the Eagles what Vonnegut did for science fiction – injected a much-needed sense of play into a staid and self-important institution.

See: *Cat's Cradle* by Kurt Vonnegut
      But Seriously, Folks... by Joe Walsh

Charles Dickens = Eric Clapton: Both Clapton and Dickens boast massive bodies of work that have garnered heaps of critical and commercial success. Both possess elder statesman stature, undeniable skill, and, depending on who you ask, mastery of their chosen instrument. And both are so dull as to induce an open-mouthed, drooling coma for which the only applicable accelerants almost always lead to addiction and death. But they're not anesthetizing across the board. Clapton has, on occasion, knocked out tunes so left-field stellar they almost justify his entire career ("Layla," "Bell Bottom Blues") and Dickens created a Christmas-lit icon in the character of stingy prick extraordinaire Ebenezer Scrooge (best portrayed by Michael Caine.) Dickens is long dead but I'd like to see Clapton survive a two-day lockup on Ginger Baker's South African compound with nothing but a Stratocaster for protection.

See: *A Muppet Christmas Carol*
    Layla & Other Assorted Love Songs by Derek & the Dominoes

Lou Reed = Hunter S. Thompson: Lou Reed and Dr. Thompson have more in common than just a love for popping speed like Skittles, though that's certainly part of the equation. Above anything else, these men were chroniclers. Reed soaked up New York's strung-out, sexually uninhibited underground freak culture, and Thompson documented the perversions and hypocrisies hidden beneath everything from the Kentucky Derby to a presidential campaign. They each saw grotesquerie in the American character and fought with all thirty-two teeth to expose it. Thompson's literary style, whether in his early days of reasonably straight journalism or his later, more famous flights of hash-addled fantasy, is marked by moments of wisdom achieved through digressions that are often as frightening as they are funny. Reed shares this meandering tendency. The Velvet Underground were a musical watershed but what gets so often overlooked is how uncool they made it seem to know anything about music, which led to some truly great moments. The guitar solo in "Pale Blue Eyes," for example, just sounds *wrong*. The guitar line's rhythm has no relationship to the song proper and is likely in a different key altogether, but somehow that dissonance wraps the song into the neat little package it's supposed to be. If the solo in a love song feels wrong, it could be because the song's creator is making a statement about love itself.

See: *Fear & Loathing on the Campaign Trail '72* by Hunter S.
    Thompson
    The Velvet Underground by the Velvet Underground

Truman Capote = Eddie Van Halen: Some words ago, I accused Capote of a 'deficiency of soul.' He's a good writer and the claim was kind of a cheap shot, though not without some merit. But read these lines from his maiden novel *Other Voices, Other Rooms* and decide for yourself:

> *"Only hypocrites would hold a man responsible for what he loves, emotional illiterates and those of righteous envy, who, in their agitated concern, mistake so frequently the arrow pointing to heaven for the one that leads to hell."*

Perfect writing is hard to find but this comes scarily close. Reading it fills me with enough awe to choke and die on.

-June, 2016

A Toyota's a Toyota

THAT THE MAJORITY OF THE POPULACE VIEWS "Weird Al" Yankovic as a novelty act is a lowdown shame. It's true that we would likely have never heard of him if not for his parodies of hits by the likes of Michael Jackson and Madonna, but to summarize him simply as a parody does the man a staggering injustice. Yankovic goes for the yucks, sure – but he's a serious artist. And like all serious artists, he's persevered through feast and famine. His ambition didn't exactly correlate with each new album but it certainly culminated with 2014's *Mandatory Fun*. *Mandatory Fun* is Al's last record with RCA, with whom he had decided not to renew his contract, and his first Billboard no. 1, capping off a decades-long catalogue of hit singles, experiments, and occasional misfires.

But Yankovic's hits are just a fraction of the story. Below, I'll explore three songs casual Al listeners probably overlooked but time will hopefully treat fairly.

* * * * *

"I'm So Sick of You" (*Bad Hair Day*, 1996) It might have seemed a little anachronistic at the time to do a *This Year's Model*-style parody long after Elvis Costello had reinvented himself many times over, but this is part of Yankovic's skill as an interpreter. For Costello fans that remember his late '70s punk and new wave output, it's a spot-on homage. For the rest, it's just a freakishly catchy breakup synth-rock tune. The song doesn't parody one particular Costello number, but instead faithfully recreates E.C's whole *modus operandi* during this period. This is especially tricky on the musical end, since Costello's Attractions were one of the most crack backing bands of the era. But Al and the boys more than do it justice, nailing the nuances, especially those of the rhythm section that made E.C and his Attractions one of the most sophisticated pop provocateurs of their time. The song is a laundry-list kiss-off letter and a perfect display of Al's ability to study and master the style of any artist who piques his interest.

"It's All About the Pentiums" (*Running with Scissors*, 1999)
This parody of Puff Daddy's "It's all About the Benjamins" was one of Yankovic's earliest forays into legitimate hip-hop and, let's be honest, the odds were stacked against him. He is, by any measure, resoundingly Caucasian. Recording the song was a bold move and it's paid dividends many times over. Since then, he's won the praise of Chamillionaire, who said of Yankovic's "Ridin'" parody, "White and Nerdy": "He's actually rapping pretty good on it, it's crazy … I didn't know he could rap like that." Nor did the world, until "It's All About the Pentiums." Assuming the role of every company's loathed-but-necessary IT guy, Al taunts those of us woefully unlearned in technology. And while he's usually a pretty safe listening for the whole family, this track contains the most savage burn in his entire catalogue: "I should do the world a favor and cap you like Old Yeller / You're

just about as useless as JPEGs to Helen Keller." Damn, Al.
Just...Damn.

"Bob" (*Poodle Hat*, 2003) The parodic depths of "Bob" are two-
fold. First, with his natural vocal inflection, Al is born Bob Dylan
impersonator. Second, he skewers the often nonsensical lyrics
that remain a hallmark of Dylan's work. And what better way to
do this than to exclusively use palindromes as lyrics? Some
samples: "Lisa Bonet ate no basil / Warsaw was raw / Was it a
car or a cat I saw?" or "God, a red nugget! A fat egg under a
dog! / Go hang a salami, I'm a lasagna hog!" Again, it's a style
parody, something Al has gotten better and better at as his career
has moved forward. But among these, "Bob" is a milestone, a
work that requires careful listening from us, deep planning from
Al, and a deep knowledge of American English's many
idiosyncrasies from us all. Also, keep in mind that Dylan's first
name is a palindrome itself, adding just another layer to Al's keen
eye for even the subtlest joke.

-August, 2016

It Might Get Meta

"Here is where a critic might count. Putting the pieces together, trying to understand what is novel and adventurous, what is enervated and complacent, can give us an idea of how much room there is in this musical culture, and in American culture – an idea of what a singer and a band can do with a set of songs mixed into the uncertainty that is the pop audience. Looking back into the corners, we might discover whose America we are living in at any moment, and where it came from. With luck, we might even touch that spirit of place Americans have always sought, and in the seeking have created."
-Greil Marcus, *Mystery Train*

THERE'S A SCENE IN CAMERON CROWE'S 2000 FILM *Almost Famous* in which the story's protagonist, a fifteen-year-old aspiring rock journalist, is embarking upon his first assignment: Interviewing Black Sabbath for *Creem* Magazine in 1973. But when our boy William tries to get backstage through the concert hall's loading dock, he is rebuffed by the lumbering doorman, a character as smug and unsympathetic as any filmic gatekeeper. Just as William is about to admit defeat, a tour bus pulls to banshee-screeching halt behind him. Aboard is Stillwater, the night's opening band, and they're running late. As the band and its manager bang on the backstage door screaming to be let in, William spies an opportunity.

Introducing himself as a journalist for *Creem*, he tells the band he'd like to interview them. "We play for the fans, not the critics," one member tells him with a condescending wave bye-bye. Another outright calls him The Enemy. So William plays the absolute last card in his hand. Addressing each member by name, he tells them how much he loves the band and praises their latest single. "And Russell," he says to the guitarist, "the guitar sound is...incendiary. *Incendiary*. Way to go."

He turns to leave and the band members share a stunned, silent moment before calling after him, practically in unison. "Don't stop there," one says. "Hey, I'm incendiary too, man," calls another, a swindler's grin on full display. And with that, Stillwater ushers William backstage, no longer The Enemy but an honored guest.

The scene is funny, as it's meant to be. But it's also a near-perfect illustration of a dynamic familiar to anyone who's ever been employed as a music journalist or been a success-hungry rock 'n' roll musician. As it happens, I've been both. But as the drummer for the ever-so-politely-reviewed Shallow Palace, I was a musician first and – try as I might – it's not easy to discard all that I've learned from touring, gigging, and grinding away in the interest of journalistic objectivity. By the nature of my experiences and the people who were there with me, the line between Artist and Critic is bound to fray from time to time. For some, the difference is as obvious as that between the sun and the moon.

It reminds me of a conversation I had with a prominent local musician some five-or-so years ago when I told him I had started doing 'the music journalism thing.' I expected him to spit into my bourbon but he actually perked up, visibly excited. "That's great," he said. When I asked him why, he just laughed. "Because, man, it's like we just snuck one of our own behind enemy lines." I didn't and still don't share that sentiment, but I get where he was coming from. There's no shortage of bands and artists, from your arena-hopping megastars to local dive bar heroes, who tend to regard the music press like one might an unfamiliar Doberman – assume the beast is hostile until it proves otherwise. Unless an anti-media posture is central to an artist's persona or they happen to be so self-actualized they've evolved into the human equivalent of a long, hot yawn, everyone would prefer to be liked.

But it's the extra-insular artist-critic relationship that interests me the most. They exist predominantly in mid-sized urban enclaves where the precise role of the local music press is a relevant subject for debate and where the lines between journalist and subject, "enemy" and "ally," are often too blurry to be clearly defined. Of course, this can only happen in places with enough artistic goings-on to merit regular coverage. Places like Columbia, to choose a completely random example.

Few in town have had more first-hand experience with this dynamic than Jordan Lawrence, the Arts & Entertainment editor at Columbia's *Free Times*. He began covering music in 2007 at *The Daily Tar Heel*, the University of North Carolina's student paper. After graduating in 2010 he freelanced for several publications in the Raleigh-Durham-Chapel Hill Triangle, even pulling a writing/editing stint at the now-defunct *Shuffle*. Unsurprisingly, his view on music journalism's role in its community is clear-cut. "I think it serves two essential purposes," he says. "The first is to the reader – that is, not the artist. I don't necessarily see it as a way to pick and choose what you listen to but as a way to think about it and hopefully gain a greater understanding of what exactly this song or artist is. Taking in the perspectives and critical opinions of people with genuine knowledge and deep understanding of the work and the way that it fits into associated genres can help anyone understand it better. On the artist's end, I see what we do as a way to understand and appreciate and take into whatever account a given artist wants compared to what kind of response the art is actually getting." On his desire to have as many different opinions as possible represented within the Free Times pages, Lawrence says, "I've built a staff of people who live here [in Columbia] and are in bands, live here and aren't in bands, and people who don't live here at all and therefore have a totally unique perspective. All points of view are important if we're going to do the job we need to do."

These approaches are totally reasonable from a journalistic standpoint, but dustups can certainly arise when artists believe they aren't being judged by a critic with any understanding of their work, much less a deep one. Such an incident occurred last November when *Free Times* published separate blurbs about local bands Dr. Roundhouse and lowercase gods, authored by contributors Ony Ratsimbaharison and myself, respectively. Taking umbrage with what he saw as disrespect towards bands he likes and considers friends, Bubbs Ruebella of local punk-metal band Pig Head Dog brought his grievances to (where else?) social media, where he was joined by a chorus of voices agreeing that much of Columbia's music coverage was unfair, elitist, and perhaps even harmful to the music community.

"We need you guys as much as you need us," Ruebella says over the telephone, glad to be spreading his message but detectably wary of me in most every way possible. "Your job is to critique and our job is to listen if it happens to concern us." But while he claims to see the artist/critic relationship as, at best, a hyper-attentive parasite trying to dig up dirt on artists who only want to do their thing, his strongest belief is that seeing a band or artist in a live setting should be a prerequisite for criticism. Before I can ask if he's ever heard of *Sergeant Pepper*, he gets to his core principle: "I'm a firm believer in live music...you can listen to a tape or a CD or whatever's online all day, but you aren't getting the purest expression of who an artist or band is unless you take the time to go see them perform live."

Ruebella isn't wrong, exactly. In an ideal situation, every rock writer would experience every act he or she writes about through every possible medium. This is impractical for a number of reasons but it's hard to argue against his larger point. If, as a musician, you feel the strongest connection to your work when performing it live, it should stand to reason that a listener would be best served experiencing it the same way. And Ruebella isn't just a punk rock shitkicker reciting the ethos. Emboldened by the knowledge that so many others shared his frustrations, Ruebella organized Fringe Fest, which will take place at Art Bar on February 18 and exclusively feature acts he feels have been mistreated or overlooked by Columbia's music journalists. Bands include cat fetishists Turbo Gatto, vintage rock act The Berries, Dr. Roundhouse, and his own Pig Head Dog. Whether these bands really are victims of the Rock Journalism Industrial Complex is highly contestable, but organizing an event whose sole purpose is promoting inter-band solidarity is without a doubt one of the most proactive things Ruebella could have done in response.

But for all of the teeth-gnashing over a know-nothing press, there are just as many artists whose attitudes land somewhere between ambivalence and appreciation. "I think a lot of times people read music journalism as if it's set in stone or as if the writer's opinion is anything more than that," says Dylan Dickerson of rock trio Dear Blanca. "I feel like music journalism is supposed to be a sort of cull for conversation. It's not supposed to be a final critique on anything…The fact that people are talking about music and art at all is something I appreciate whether it's positive or negative." Of course, it's easy to mosey along the high road when you've never really been on the business end of a critical thwacking, and from the moment the band's first proper record appeared in 2013, Dear Blanca has amassed little but the highest praise from local and regional publications. Though he hasn't received much himself, Dickerson knows well that there's no such thing as bad press. "If anything," he continues, "a lot of people have thrived in the wake of negative publicity. If the press doesn't like your stuff, then that's as much of a reason or people to check it out than if you were getting five-star reviews left and right. Maybe sometimes if you read something that you feel is railing against a band or artist and being really unfair, you'd be more inclined to check it out for yourself."

These sorts of mini-controversies have happened countless times in countless cities and they're not going anywhere. Friction and disagreement are baked into the artist/critic relationship. But it's important to remember that the kid who picks up a guitar because she knows she's got a song somewhere inside of her has more in common than she realizes with the kid who finds himself curious not so much about the song's origin but its eventual place in the world. At some point, these kids fell in love with the same thing and want to know all that it's capable of accomplishing, from the pedestrian to the majestic to the incendiary.

-April, 2017

Covering

IF YOU RESENT HAVING THE OBVIOUS POINTED OUT TO you, well, so do I. But there's a time and place for everything and this paragraph is one of them, so let me begin with a couple of things most of us likely know already: A rock band needs at least one guitar (preferably electric, with a nice crunchy sound) and typically (but not necessarily) a bass guitar, a drum set, and a singer (not required, but always the smart decision.) Piano or keyboard isn't uncommon and can give your rock band a nice, bouncy quality, if that's the sort of thing you want. Saxophone is sort of novel these days but not unheard-of, though there was a time when no rock band left home without it. But whichever instruments you've got at your disposal, remember to keep'em loud. Nothing facilitates a fever transference between rock band and rock audience quite like generous volume. Deafening noise can also mask any performance issues that may arise, especially if your rock band is a shitty one. But 'rock' also functions quite well as a verb. In theory, it's not just music to be listened to but something we all have the potential to do. Exceptionally well-prepared breakfast foods have even been known to rock. But simply being a rock band doesn't guarantee the band will rock. The Doobie Brothers and Matchbox 20 are good examples of this.

* * * * *

The band I'm covering may not check every single box but nevertheless meets the requisite criteria. Having existed right here in this very city for about five years, the band I'm covering is a rock band – but not *just* a rock band. The band I'm covering is a rock band that not only rocks, but rocks hard, and that not only rocks hard, but kicks ass. **And despite rumors to the contrary**, rocking hard and kicking ass are not the same thing. A rock band that can't manage the former should do itself a favor and forget all about the latter. This isn't a kiddie game. Lives have been destroyed in the pursuit of what the band I'm covering is and does.

Their music has been regularly exalted in the press and on the street. The most common sentiment about the band I'm covering is that, as far as local music goes, they wrote the book on rocking hard whilst kicking ass. You might think that such high praise would be a point of pride for the band I'm covering. You might even worry about it going to their heads. Or perhaps what we all see as a rare and special gift is for them a source of untenable pressure and their private hell on earth. Any of these scenarios are possible, but not one of them is true.

I meet the lead singer of the band I'm covering at the agreed-upon tavern at the agreed-upon time. We shake hands and make small talk until our beer arrives. I turn on my tape recorder and the interview, such as it is, begins in earnest. The band I'm covering is about to release its third record and anticipation is high not just in this city, but others all across the region. The upcoming record is the reason I'm interviewing the lead singer at all, but first I ask him how he feels about his band's ability to both rock hard and kick ass to the highest possible degree. He starts to say something but cuts himself off with a brief, smarmy grin. He has an answer to this question but it's not something I or my tape recorder are going to hear. So instead of giving me the actual answer, he grasps for something that resembles it, knowing that if he ignores me I'll just ask him the same thing again. "We play rock, but it's outsider rock," he says, apparently starting an entirely new, separate conversation. He takes a beat, gauging how he feels about the statement he just made, unsure if he believes it. Either way, he continues, "It's for people that kick ass but don't know how to exist within mainstream culture."

I'm about to ask what he means by 'mainstream culture,' but something about his face gives me pause. His body language communicates just the right amount of nonchalance and an acceptable amount of cockiness, but there's nothing he can do about the terror flickering across his eyes, if he's even aware of it. I've seen it before in many of the musicians I've interviewed, and I think I know what it means. It means he's over it. Over *this*. He doesn't like people with tape recorders asking him any question they please, taking for granted that he'll answer it at all. I almost feel sorry for him but it passes. I ask him what he means by 'mainstream culture.' He demurs, pretending to think it over. But I know what he's really thinking. He's wondering whether I'm here to help him or hurt him. He's wondering if I privately like his band. He's wondering if and when the big publications come knocking he'll look like an asshole if he refuses interviews with local papers, even though he'd like to. He's wondering why I'm bothering with him at all when the music itself could tell me everything I need to know better than he ever could. He's wondering if all of the things that are meant to happen for him will happen at all. And if they don't, he's wondering what the hell he's supposed to do then.

We order another round of beer and the lead singer tells me what mainstream culture means to him, which illuminates nothing. I ask a few more questions about the band I'm covering's upcoming record and subsequent tour and then abruptly turn the tape recorder off. The lead singer seems confused, as if maybe he said the wrong thing and upset me, not knowing there is no such thing as 'saying the wrong thing' as far as an interview is concerned. We shake hands and I thank him for his time. He thanks me in return but doesn't say why. We both leave the tavern and wave the wave of good buddies before getting into our cars and driving home, where we each dig out the value in the evening's conversation until panic sets in and then paralyzes us completely, just as it does every time.

-September, 2017

Black Hole Music

Y MISSION, AS I UNDERSTAND IT, IS TO SHARE my thoughts regarding my time in Shallow Palace, a Columbia-based rock band that existed from 2005 to 2017 and played its final show the day before my thirty-first birthday. I shouldn't be too maudlin or too cocky about our adventures. I should avoid clichés (such as the old saw that a self-funded rock 'n' roll tour is tough but rewarding) while giving the truth its due (a self-funded rock 'n' roll tour is tough but rewarding.)

At least they gave me a word limit.

A scattered, mostly chronological history: Greg Slattery, Andy Auvil, and I start playing in the dining room of my rented house on Laurens Street and our live debut is a Battle of the Bands hosted by a Christian college. Jesus, apparently unmoved by punkish ditties about girls and driving, sends us packing. Josh Bumgarner joins the band on guitar. We tape an appearance on MTV in baggy-eyed shambles after a night of underage carousing on the streets of Manhattan. We return home to no fanfare and are compared in the local press to Nirvana, the Stooges, Muse, the Beatles, and the MC5 (though not all at once, and the Beatles thing didn't seem sincere or at all complimentary.) Brett Kent joins the band, replacing Andy on

bass. George Fish joins on guitar and keys, replacing no one.
Our first album is a little too long but has a handful of good
songs I still enjoy today. It sells accordingly and we go on an east
coast tour to see how many strangers dig what we're doing. We
record and tour again, record and tour again, and so on and so
forth. Things begin to stagnate. We've been at this a while with
few financial or existential merit badges to show for the work.
Brett makes his exit, followed shortly by Josh. Replacing Brett is
Ameer Raja, chosen for his skill and the Shallow Palace tattoo he
insists he doesn't regret. We discuss replacing Josh but a guffaw is
heard from on high and the subject is never revisited. We play a
few more shows before admitting to ourselves that this thing has
run its course. Brett and Josh agree to one last hurrah and Ameer
steps aside like the goddam gentleman he is. Our final show is at
Art Bar and we play to one of the biggest and best audiences we
have ever drawn there. "That went about as well as it could
have," I think afterward, any lingering illusions of youth and
stardom now shovel-smacked under cold dirt.

I'm not interested in convincing any reader who hasn't
heard of the band that they missed out on something magical. I'd
actually be impressed they made it this far. But hokey as it may
sound, there were moments where that's kind of what it was. For
me, anyway, and I think the others would say something similar.
I spent twelve years of my life writing, playing, and causing
untold damage to my eardrums with guys I'll consider brothers
until I can no longer consider. There were countless times in the
van, the studio, or the practice space where we couldn't even
look one another in the eye, much less get through a
conversation without slinging shit. But that's not what I'm going
to see clearest when I look back.

I'm going to see Greg doing a whole east coast run in a cast because he broke his arm practicing David Lee Roth kicks in the kitchen. I'm going to see Maurice, the lonely, middle-aged man who let us crash in his Massachusetts basement and had been struggling with severe depression since his daughter moved out. I hope he is alive and happy. I'm going to see George behind the wheel of the van in the middle of the night, the two of us the only ones still awake as snowflakes gather outside, explaining to me that if a person were somehow able to stand at the edge of a black hole they'd be able to witness the beginning and end of all creation, all in one moment, and then debating what song we would want to be playing if we ever got to see it ourselves. I think we settled on something by Queen. I'm going to remember being on a New York City subway car as 2008 became 2009 and then waking up freezing on the floor of the van, parked on a Polish street in Brooklyn. I'll remember all of the inside jokes and how hard we laughed, knowing we were speaking a language no one else could penetrate. I'll remember the safety in knowing that no matter what happened, I was in it with people I loved and trusted.

We could have been any anonymous rock band in the world. I'll be grateful forever.

-October, 2017

PART III

WHERE PRAYER SALTS THE AIR

Reverend Mickens Shouts at the Devil

"Man cannot judge it. For art sings of God and ultimately belongs to him." -
Patti Smith

IT'S HIGH NOON IN COLUMBIA. REVEREND MICKENS AND the new Highway Travelers take the stage right on time, resplendent in matching suits of deep and unnatural blue. After some perfunctory tuning and futzing with amplifiers, the Travelers – Mickens' sons Justin, Colton, and Todd (electric guitar, bass guitar, and drums, respectively), and nephew Jamie (keys) – launch into the opening number. It's a high-energy appeal to heaven and the band's chops are tighter than the jaws of life. You can feel Todd's bass drum in your footwear and Justin's high notes mingle easily with the indecisive wind. The 2014 Jam Room Music Festival has officially begun.

The early crowd, though attentive, is sparse. But lunchtime malaise be damned, Reverend Mickens and his progeny command those assembled with the same authority one imagines they would a Sunday morning congregation packed to the scaffolding. Even for an audience that might not give half a damn about Jesus the Christ and his whole bloody tale, the Travelers have a lot to offer. They're not only proficient musicians and singers (four-part harmony is executed with precision), but highly skilled showmen. Justin and Colton Mickens frequently break out a little tandem soft-shoe, always in step with one another, never missing a note.

The audience grows steadily as the set rolls on and by the last song – a smoldering cover of Sam Cooke's "A Change is Gonna Come," – a now-crowded Main Street has the palpable, electric aura of mass conversion – if not to the band's ham-fisted message of faith and spirituality, then at least to the Travelers themselves. It's unclear whether any souls were saved during the fifty-minute set but there's no doubting that Reverend Mickens and the New Highway Travelers kicked off the festival in high style.

They're the *New* Highway Travelers for a reason. The band's precursor, simply named the Highway Travelers, formed in 1964 in Hopkins, South Carolina and consisted of a much younger Matthew Mickens and his twelve siblings. "It was a family group with me and my sisters and brothers," remembers Mickens. "It was actually our mama that named us the Highway Travelers. And after a few year of singing and performing, we all got a little bit older and went our separate ways." But it was in 1999 that Mickens caught the bug again and set about getting the band back together. "I was singing in church as part of the choir but that wasn't letting me stretch out musically like I wanted to. What I really wanted was to get back to leading a gospel band," he says. So, along with one of his brothers, they formed the New Highway Travelers. After an ever-revolving door of family members joining and leaving the group, Reverend Mickens finally found a solid backup ensemble in his sons and nephew, the line-up that remains today. Together, they've released five full-length albums, the most recent being 2012's *He*

Paid the Cost. A follow-up (or at least a plan for a follow-up) is already underway.

The Reverend, 62, has a deep, soulful, mint-condition singing voice, along with all the weary charisma you'd expect from a man who draws his water turning up the temperature in crowded rooms. He's been preaching professionally since he was ordained in 1989 and couldn't fake stage fright if you paid him – not that it matters. Money seems to hold little interest for the Reverend and he sees himself performing exclusively for an audience of one. "People have different ears for different things but what we try to do is, I just want the people to know that there's another way," he says. "But God is the one. We sing and dance and have a good time. We want other people to have a good time too, of course. But the most important thing is getting people away from a lifestyle that might not be so good for them. The world does its thing and we do ours. I just happened to think our thing is better. Way better," he adds with a smirk. "I work for the lord before anyone else."

Good music is good music and a great show is likewise just that. But while plenty of Christian artists have dined out on a record-buyer's possible ambivalence toward a higher message by downplaying the book and pumping up the hook, gospel has no such luxury. It may sound like a simple point, but there really is no secular gospel. Hope and faith are wrapped up in its very DNA. A vision of god is burned deep into its marrow. That isn't to say that gospel music is some subterranean cultural Fight Club appreciated only by a zealous few sworn not to discuss it with outsiders. Aretha Franklin is recognized as one the greatest singers in human history and choirmaster general Kirk Franklin (no relation) is sitting on seven Grammys. Even Elton John hired a choir and scored a minor hit in 1970 with the hymnal "Border

Song," in which finds John pleads for equality. Gospel choirs have been appearing in the background of a host of pop songs over the years, most recently on Sam Smith's smash ballad, "Stay with Me." But these exceptions only illuminate the larger rule. The hard fact is that gospel just doesn't have the crossover appeal necessary to be a commercially competitive genre in a society that grows more secular with every passing day.

But that might be beside the point.

"It's not really about winning awards or getting into the Top 40," says Colton Mickens. "It's about reaching someone or helping someone get closer to god. I mean, you can reach a lot of people when you're sitting pretty on the charts but it's not like everybody has that chance."

What's so interesting about gospel music is that, as opposed to other popular music forms, it's almost totally immune to critical deconstruction. The nuances that typically make a song, an album, or a performance good or bad, as these terms are usually understood, are useless when it comes to gospel. This is a wholly American genre born out of the sincerest joy and the most deeply embedded pain, and the people for whom it exists – the ones that not only love and are moved by it, but depend on it – aren't working up a sweat just to prove that it's hot. Gospel numbers aren't judged by a hook, interesting chord formations, or a lack of treble. Its purpose is higher.

"I'm in the god business," says Reverend Mickens. "The music business can take care of itself, but god - that's forever."

-December, 2014

Indecent Man

With a cowboy hat doffed above a pair of dark sunglasses, at least one Marlboro dangling from his lips, and a star-spangled, red-white-and-blue button-down, he's impossible to miss in a crowd. He walks with a lazy swagger, well aware that the party won't start until he gets there and won't end until they carry him out. Once he takes the stage, get ready to have your mind melt from your ears like a candle in the Tucson sun. Like what you hear? You're welcome. He's Danny Joe Machado, and if you think he's crushing it now, you should have seen him in 1974.

"**H**E'S AN ASSHOLE MUSICIAN WITH delusions of grandeur," says Daniel Machado, 31, explaining his latest and most mercurial creation. "I've only ever played in a local music scene and it's amazing how many people are absolutely full of themselves, are convinced they're great, think that you should think they're great, and act accordingly kind of across the board. I just thought it might be kind of interesting to embody that character a little bit, to bring the actual identity into the project itself. And I think as creative people, this Danny Joe character is something we all need to be wary of."

As primary frontman and songwriter for local band the Restoration, Machado is no neophyte when it comes to writing from fictional perspectives. On the band's 2010 conceptual watershed *Constance*, a multi-generational family drama set in the antebellum South, he acted as the mouthpiece for a slew of personalities that could have easily been ripped from Faulkner. Two years later, the band released *Honor the Father*, where Machado stepped into the role of religious zealot and certifiable sociopath Roman Bright. Dedicated to plot and chronology as well as character, they were stories best told through the words, thoughts, and actions of the folks that inhabited them, all set to some of Machado's most accomplished songwriting to date.

Danascus, his first release under the Danny Joe moniker, is something different. The record isn't so much a narrative as a character exercise, a vehicle for Machado's writing in the guise of his unsavory alter ego. But *Danascus* isn't a one-note joke. Danny Joe might appear to be little more than a comic parody of rock star douchebaggery, but the album that bears his name is just as complex and fully-realized as any of Machado's other, more 'serious-minded' efforts. Songs like "Nineteen Seventy-Three," a high-spirited rocker celebrating the singer's bygone glory days, and "Decent Man," an insistent defense of his indefensible behavior, are the personality at work. But the real Daniel Machado – the one whose intellectual property staggers and struts across *Danascus'* thirteen tracks – remains a vital presence. The line between creator and creation is blurred here, there, and everywhere, a point Machado readily concedes.

"The way it was put together was kind of a piggybacking, alternating thing," he says. "There are songs on the album that I know are way more where I'm coming from and songs that I know are way more where he's coming from. Songs like "Hymn" and "Nobody Cares" are pretty straightforwardly me." As for the notion that the self-absorption so integral to Danny Joe's personality might be at odds with the occasional winking self-mockery in the lyrics, Machado isn't particularly bothered. "I like the idea that people who are, on the surface, or appear a certain way on the surface, they, well – Danny Joe might not necessarily be self-aware the way the lyrics of certain songs might make him out to be."

If the Danny Joe character is to be viewed as cautionary for artists, especially musicians, as Machado claims, what exactly is he cautioning against?

Like the late Andy Kaufman's blowhard lounge singer alter ego Tony Clifton, Danny Joe is a glorious farce, a perfectly executed example of a man whose only charge is to entertain but consistently runs afoul of likeability. But where Kaufman was out to amuse only himself, more than happy to let the audience speculate for years on his association with Clifton, Machado would never be so duplicitous. He lets us in on the game immediately. The Danny Joe act lasts before, during, and after a given performance because the costume and persona are only pieces of the equation. We have Danny Joe, elegantly wasted up on the stage, but we also have *Danascus*, an artifact we can take home an enjoy long after last call. We're not supposed to root for the character the same way we appreciate the musical product. When we clap and cheer for the Tony Cliftons and the Danny Joes, we're really cheering for their creators' mastery over the dark art of shape-shifting. We're cheering for the public spectacle of a full-grown boob of a man pretending he's anything but.

It's telling that early promotional material for *Danascus* billed it as 'The solo project nobody asked for,' and, later, 'The biggest flop since 1973.' This could be written off as self-deprecation on

Machado's part, but it speaks to a larger truth about this particular type of performance art. The record is excellent and deserves all the success and attention it can get, but the same can't be said for Danny Joe. We know it, Machado knows it, and, for all of his puckish bluster, Danny Joe knows it. Though Machado would never claim himself any sort of moral arbiter, Danny Joe could well be the once-talented schmuck reminding other artists of the dangers of egotism, the takeaway here being that old parabolic saw about unchecked pride giving way to a disastrous collapse. Danny Joe has to fail. He must collapse. His other half's basic decency demands it.

But this incongruity between the high quality of the album and the obtusely inept character that inhabits it creates an interesting dilemma for Daniel Machado. As of now, he doesn't have any plans to record further under the Danny Joe name because, at present, there's no real pressure to do so. At the very least, *Danascus* is sure to do well within South Carolina. But what it went further, gaining traction on a much bigger scale? This is the sort of question most artists would hardly consider a dilemma, but Daniel Machado isn't most artists. What if he awoke one morning to find his chain-smoking, hard-drinking, satyriasis-afflicted alter ego in high commercial demand? Basically, what if he had to be Danny Joe *every night*?

Faced with this improbable but not impossible scenario, Machado takes reflective pause. "If that were a real situation," he says, lowering his eyes, "it would be a horrifying nightmare."

-October, 2015

The Rap on Mark

"Funny story," Mark Rapp says, flashing some of the whitest teeth I've ever seen. "I went to a party at Marsalis' house in New York, like I did a lot. You know, I'd come over a lot and we'd play chess and shoot the shit. Anyway, Laurence Fishburne is at this party. And I'm talking with a group of guys, you know – jazz musicians. We're talking about girls and things like that. Fishburne overhears and walks over to us and says, 'Young men, let me tell you something.' Of course we're all like, 'Of course, yeah, Mr. Fishburne. What do you have to say?' I won't go into the whole thing but basically he was talking about how to treat a woman with respect to the point where she will not let you leave the apartment. Like, she's gonna throw you down on the bed and just ravish you because of how lovingly and respectfully you've been treating her. And at one point in the story he's like, 'And then what you do is, you get a bubble bath going and some flowers and stuff and lay her on the bed and kiss her goodnight.' Then he leaned in and kissed me on the forehead to demonstrate. And then he walked away. And we're all like, 'Wait a minute! You don't make love or anything?' He just turns around and says, 'That's the point. She will never let you leave that apartment again.'

"Laurence Fishburne kissed me on the forehead at Wynton Marsalis' house. That might be a pretty good opening for your article, man."

THE LIGHTING IS DIM, AS IT ALWAYS IS. HIGHBALL glasses clink in the background, as they always do. Side conversation is muted, per the venue's unspoken code of conduct. It's a Thursday night at Delaney's Speakeasy and local jazz is the evening's main attraction.

In the open floorspace before the fireplace, in clear view of anyone lounging on the plush sofas and chairs or protecting hard-won real estate at the bar, Mark Rapp is leading his band through an interpretation of John Williams' "Imperial March," better known as Darth Vader's leitmotif in the *Star Wars* films. Before the piece begins, Rapp admits that he's been drinking a little bit and asks us for some slack. Maybe it's the drink, maybe it's jazz's improvisational nature, but the selection doesn't begin as any great shakes. There are false starts that elicit good-natured laughter from the band but the audience hangs in there. Undeterred, Rapp charges through and conducts his backing trio through the introduction. Finally, the tune takes recognizable shape and lands with authority. The rhythm now firmly secured, Rapp joins in on his trumpet. Vader has arrived from a galaxy far, far away, as a jazz cat of the highest and darkest order. The shakiness of the past few moments are forgotten and we're now in the thick of a performance emblematic of the sort of artist that Mark Rapp is. He's a conductor, a composer, an interpreter, a reluctant perfectionist, and – above all – a ravenous fan. Put bluntly, Mark Rapp is a mega-talented, over-enthused jazz geek.

Seated nearby with drained glass in hand, I'm consumed by two thoughts: 1) Drinking is way more fun when we pretend it's still prohibited and 2) Mark Rapp plays his trumpet the same way he eats his lunch.

* * * * *

Hours earlier, Mark Rapp, 33, and I are seated across from one
another in a corner booth at Delaney's, the companion Irish Pub
to the jazz joint where he will later perform. Rapp is hungry and
requests a turkey avocado wrap. When his food arrives, he leaves
it untouched for what seems like a quarter decade but is really
only about fifteen, maybe twenty minutes. Finally, he reaches
down and picks off the smallest possible piece. There is no meat,
no avocado, and no lettuce – only a morsel of flour tortilla. The
interview is now a million miles away as he eats, not so much
chewing as grazing. After several more minutes, he repeats the
action. We're nearly a half hour into our conversation and he
still hasn't taken anything that could be called a 'bite.' At the risk
of sounding over-dramatic, it's driving me bonkers. *Dig in, Rapp!* I
scream inside. *Life is short! Entire nations are starving to death! Do the
damn thing!* This pick-and-chew routine goes on and on until, at
last, he picks up the wrap and tears into it like Hannibal Lector
did that security guard.

Watching him play later I realize that Mark Rapp tackles
his lunch like he tackles performance. He begins with caution,
getting a feel for the piece. He settles into a groove and allows the
music to evolve, to develop an identity. He test-runs a few notes
until they gel with the larger composition. Then and only then,
when he's satisfied with the state of things, he picks up his
trumpet (or wrap, or whatever) and plunges in, squashing any
doubt that he came not to play around, but to *play*.

* * * * *

With his horn-rimmed glasses and clean-living aura, Mark Rapp vaguely resembles Weezer's Rivers Cuomo. He also indulges liberally in the sort of eyebrow gymnastics that make me think he's got a pretty decent Christian Slater impression tucked away in his repertoire. But his defining non-musical characteristic is that he's a consummate raconteur. When narrating his career's trajectory, he moves easily between adult self-awareness and boyish enthusiasm, neither appearing forced or in the service of a persona. Like any good story, his contains a hero who faces trials and tribulations. He falls in love, but this only leads to self-doubt. After more failure, he much choose between giving up or taking fate into his own hands. Our hero chooses the latter and in doing so finds redemption and restores the social order. But those are the Cliffs Notes.

These are the facts: Rapp was born in Rockledge, Florida and, when he was three, the family moved to Florence, South Carolina. He pursued higher learning at Winthrop University, earning a Bachelor's degree in Music Performance. It was around this time that Rapp had his 'ah-ha!' moment, that epiphany every artist has when the clouds suddenly part to reveal his or her personal Holy Grail – that which is out of reach for now but very much in sight.

"A buddy of mine had a funk band," Rapp says, eyebrows bobbing and weaving like Joe Frazier, "and he was like, 'I want some horns in my funk band.' So I came to a rehearsal and I'm looking for the sheet music like, 'What do I play?' He goes, 'Naw, man. Just improvise. Make it up." I didn't know what he was talking about. Like, no idea. So he said, 'Alright, man' and he took me back to his house and says, 'You ever hear of Louis Armstrong? Miles Davis? John Coltrane? Dexter Gordon?' He started playing these records for me and it was incredible. That's how I fell in love with jazz, man." It was a revelation that led to the most significant relationship of Rapp's early career. "So I dove in head-deep," he goes on. "That's when I met Wynton Marsalis. Man. Anytime he was within an eight-hour drive, I was at his shows. I was following him like crazy. I would sneak back stage, try to meet the band. I did that constantly."

In time, Rapp and Marsalis developed something of a Kenobi-Skywalker relationship, though Rapp is quick to downplay it as little more than a jazz legend humoring a young trumpeter just trying to make the scene. The elder musician dispensed advice and encouragement. The two even jammed together on occasion. Emboldened by Marsalis' confidence in him, Rapp moved to New Orleans. He spent about five years in the city playing music, partying, and working on his Master's degree in Jazz. He recalls the period fondly. "It was an incredible time in terms of my foundation in jazz. Good lord, man. New Orleans has such soul, it's incredible."

After the Big Easy, it was the Big Apple, where he lived from 2000 to 2008. "That first year in New York…it was just dark, man…I remember the first jam session I went to within the first few weeks I was there. I remember it clear as day. The guys in there, they're *burning*. And I'm still thinking I can hang. This little kid walks over to a trombone that's taller than him, this dorky-looking kid, and I'm like, 'Well, if he's sitting in, I'll give it a try.' And this kid just plays the fuck out of it. So I put my horn away, went home, and cried for the next hour. I literally cried, man. I said, 'There's no way I can hang here. I'm not gonna make it.'"

But the lean times weren't to last. After a brief mental breakdown which included Rapp 'losing his lip' (meaning he couldn't play a damn thing), he eventually found a band and a regular gig in a Manhattan cigar bar just behind Carnegie Hall. In the parlance of the jazz world, Mark Rapp had finally made the hang.

His first album, *Token Tales*, appeared in 2009 and was followed by a collaboration with fellow jazz musician Don Braden under the name the Strayhorn Project. Amid this period of unprecedented productivity, Rapp fell in love with a woman, married her, and moved to her native Europe. If the story had ended there it would be a fairy tale, but those don't exist in jazz. The marriage deteriorated and Rapp returned to the U.S., settling in Columbia, SC. Still reeling from love lost, Rapp swore off music altogether. It was only through therapy that he managed to regain the confidence to not only give his passion another chance, but make a positive contribution to Columbia's jazz scene.

"I got this idea," Rapp says in a manner that's somehow both conspiratorial and enthusiastic. "I want to record all these bandleaders, all these bands. I want to highlight the talent we've got here in Columbia. Really, man. There's some world-class talent living and playing right here in Columbia. We've got Bert Ligon, Dick Goodwin, Skipp Pearson – these are legends of jazz and they're right here in our city. Then there's current cats like Reggie Sullivan, myself, Robert Gardiner, Jay Ware, Amos Hoffman...there's twenty-seven musicians we've recorded and thirteen bands." Co-produced with Jangly Records' Paul Bodamer, *Cola Jazz 2015* will be released soon, Rapp promises, though he can't give an exact date.

As a man who's lived and played in some of America's finest jazz scenes and even a few abroad, he comes by his affection for Columbia's jazz community honestly. "The scene here is small," he says, "but it's strong. There are a handful of players here that I would put up against any player in the world. There's some world-class talent here, man. And I'm hoping with the compilation CD, there will be a trickle-down effect resulting in more venues hosting more live jazz. Even if it's just a restaurant with a trio in the corner, that's something. For the size of this city, we're doing great. Really great, man."

-February, 2016

Guided by Voices

ANY DISCUSSION ABOUT FEMALE MUSICIANS IN
Columbia – or about the city's best music, period –
that doesn't include the Prairie Willows is the result of
either willful ignorance or flat-out subterfuge. On the strength of
a slim but stellar discography (2013's *Prairie Willows* and last
year's *White Lies*) and a steady track record of room-demolishing
live performances, Kristen Harris, Perrin Skinner, and Kelley
McLachlan Douglas have shed their early reputation as a
talented and promising folk trio to become a vocal ensemble
unrivaled well beyond the city limits.

"We'd all kind of been separately involved in the music
scene," recalls Perrin Skinner of the band's 2012 beginnings.
"Kelley was in Post-Timey String Band and I met Kristen
through playing with a mutual friend of ours. She moved in with
me and we all just decided to mess around and collaborate, you
know, play in the living room, and then it just became what it
became." From there, the newly formed Prairie Willows tested
the waters at open-mic nights hosted by Utopia (which has since
been shuttered), developing their chemistry and covering tunes
by Willie Nelson, Waylon Jennings, Dolly Parton, and others.

Their self-titled debut appeared in 2013. With only five
songs and a sixteen-minute running time, the record is by no

means an opus, but as a showcase for the band's celestial three-part harmonies and formidable songwriting, it did the job and then some. The opener, "Whiskey," is a minor-key ode to better living through liquor, while the playful "Biscuits" is pure mountain bluegrass bliss. And even though the Willows' catalogue is littered with forays into country and Americana, all with a deep vein of Southern Gothic storytelling, they generally write within a folk music framework. While for the most part consistent, their sound reveals a few different personalities at work. Hardly a surprise, given their creative process.

"We usually start with a melody and then spend hours trying to figure out the other two parts," says Harris. "That's usually when we get in a really big fight and go away for week. Then we come back after things have settled and we can start to tweak it."

"Typically, whoever writes the song does the melody," adds Douglas, who writes the bulk of the material before bringing it to the band in various stages of completion. Here, edges are sanded down, vocal parts arranged, structure tinkered with, meat added to the bone. "Then we might switch verses. I might lead one and then Perrin leads one and then we stack each other on top of that while Kristen takes the low." Instrumentally, Douglas and/or Skinner play acoustic guitar while Harris starts mini-fires with her fiddle.

* * * * *

If you're reading this, you're likely already aware that this publication sets aside the month of March to spotlight the achievements of Columbia's female artists. Given this, not to mention their stature among our city's musicians, covering the

Prairie Willows was a no-brainer. A cynic could argue that simply raising the issue presumes a male majority in music communities. The uncomfortable truth is that the cynic has a pretty solid point (which I guess would make this hypothetical person not a cynic, but a realist.) There isn't just one answer or solution here, and I'm reminded of the theory that, in childhood, boys are typically encouraged more in their musical interests than girls are, leading to an overwhelming majority of male musicians and critics later on. Female musicians aren't hard to come by in any community but it seems like you can't chuck a Zesto's burger in this town without hitting a guy with a guitar. None of this is right or fair. I have also, as of this writing, never raised children, so my expertise here is zero.

In any case, the saucy, Ginger Spice-ish Girl Power of the '90s is getting further behind us every day and what we're left with is something not quite as flamboyant but no less important. As the city's most prominent all-female group, some might expect the Prairie Willows to act as torchbearers of femme-folk militancy, or that the band would take upon itself the job of promoting feminist ideals. But neither seems to be the case and the band is quick to point out, with trace exasperation, how frequently they're asked to these issues. Their weariness on the subject is understandable. I feel like a schlub just bringing it up. As mentioned earlier, Douglas is also half of the power-folk duo Post-Timey String Band. Her partner is Sean Thompson (also of the Restoration), and one imagines he isn't too often asked what it's like to be a dude in a band. I know I never was.

"I feel like people want to define us as a feminist band, but that's never really been our goal," says Harris. Douglas elaborates: "Even if there are undertones of that in our lyrics, it was never intentional...we write how we feel and I think sometimes that might come across as a feminist stance, but we don't mean it that way." They may shrug off the idea of themselves as emblematic of any socio-political push, but the Prairie Willows don't downplay the importance their position might carry for certain members of their audience.

On this, Harris is customarily succinct: "If people see us and they feel like that empowers them to be in a band and perform, then I'm all about it."

-March, 2016

Live Transmission

April 15, 9:16 PM EST, NEW BROOKLAND TAVERN LIKE METALLICA, Rancid, the Dixie Chicks, and Blues Traveler before them, the Gardener and the Willow is one of those expository names that totally embody a band's sonic personality. Never mind that the Gardener and the Willow isn't a 'band' in the traditional sense. Sole member Austin Lee, presumably pulling double duty as both gardener and willow, delivers his moody, pastoral songs gently. Lyrically, they're gentle in the way that someone calmly cataloguing the ways in which you've ruined their life is gentle.

When Lee takes the stage, only a few people move for a better view. The rest hang around the bar, shoot pool, or smoke various herbs and spices on the back patio. His first song sounds lonesome but threatening. Over the crack of cue balls and cans of Pabst hissing to life, Lee's voice remains steady, undeterred, even pretty. A song or two later, Dempsey's Aaron Reece joins him onstage. They sound good together, both vocally and on dual guitar, but those about to rock are getting antsy. By the last song, Lee's voice is all but drowned out by barroom chatter and he leaves the stage as he arrived, inconspicuously and to polite applause. It's a shame and he deserves better.

From the direction of the bar, someone says what is either, "I haven't heard the Mobros in two years," or, "I haven't had Marlboros in two years." Well, friend, each is the result of choices you yourself made, but tonight could be your night to break free.

10:11 PM EST Call it the Opener's Curse. In between the Gardener and the Willow's last song and Watson Village's first, the number of bodies at New Brookland Tavern nearly doubles. The mere sight of Watson Village setting up its drum kit and tuning its guitars electrifies the air in a way that no actual song by poor Austin Lee ever did. This is a crowd is clearly ready for some good old-fashioned rocking out and Watson Village does its best to oblige.

Singer/guitarist Tyler Watson, drummer David Moody, keyboard player Zack Cameron, and bassist Tyler Phillips are off to a good start. The first tune – high-energy and heavy on the blues – serves as an antidote for the unecstatic soul-baring that came before. The follow-up, "Putty in Your Pocket," loses its way in an overlong jam that never quite finds its climax. Watson Village takes the misstep in stride and soldiers on. Game to cut loose, the audience is right there with them, strong in enthusiasm if not in sheer numbers. The back patio currently boasts the night's highest attendance so far and the bar never really empties.

<u>10:58 PM EST</u> There was a time not that long ago when the Mobros were one of the most talked-about bands in the Midlands. Not yet old enough to buy their own beer, the sibling duo was rightfully hailed as junior blues saviors, soul food you could watch ripen in real time. These claims were validated when the late B.B. King hand-picked them to open a handful of his 2013 Southeastern tour dates. Their buzz has died down a bit since then, as buzz tends to do, but spending a large chunk of the past two years on the road (as well as the addition of a touring bassist) has only tightened the chops of a band already known for its proficiency.

The world currently has more blues-rock bands than it does polar ice caps, but a traditional blues band is something altogether less common, and that's exactly what the Mobros are. Kelly Morris' singing voice carries a heft of soul usually reserved for older, wearier men. His fingers fly up and down the guitar neck with avian grace. His brother Patrick on drums is the spine, the foundation, holding the songs erect with crack timing and understated flair. The standing room is swelling to capacity now and the whole place smells like whiskey and tobacco and Old Spice Classic. This is what folks have come to see. With their button-down shirts tucked neatly into their slacks and not a hair in their mini-afros out of place, the Morris Brothers look both precocious and professional. Not showmen by nature, their live appeal rests solely in their talent and the enjoyment they don't bother to contain. From their opening song until the finale, there is no pretense of innovation, only two young men (and their bassist) doing what they've committed themselves to doing.

April 16, 12:06 AM EST The show is over and I battle the despair that comes with settling one's tab. Even a modest-sized audience can be unwieldy when everyone is trying to leave at once, but I emerge more or less intact. I make it home safely and catch a little sleep, after which I write what you have just finished reading.

-April, 2016

A Voice in the Attic

HUMANS ARE PSYCHO-ENGINEERED TO LOOK FOR order where it exists and create it ourselves where it doesn't. As much as we may not like admitting it, hierarchies form within any artistic community, spurring plenty of debate amongst its chroniclers, fans, and the artists themselves about who's creating the best stuff, who's doing the most interesting work, who conjures the most meaning out of the mundane, and whose best days can be seen waving in the rearview mirror. But when it comes to music in the Capital City, you're unlikely to hear too many serious arguments against the merits of Dear Blanca. Since its formation, the three-piece rock band has been making a steady climb to the top of the heap, and not for nothing.

Dear Blanca began in the waning months of 2011 when singer/songwriter Dylan Dickerson began using the name for his solo performances. Finding this arrangement unsatisfactory, as many do, he enlisted drummer Marc Coty to man the skins. They released the band's debut full-length *Talker* in 2013. Finally, bassist Cameron Powell climbed aboard to round things out. As a trio, Dear Blanca released *Pobrecito* the following year, fulfilling what bits of promise existed on *Talker*. *Pobrecito* was the work of a band still growing into maturity while giving off the impression of believing itself fully-formed, or at least pretty close. It was, and is, a damn good record. Rife with urgency and passion from the first track, *Pobrecito* signaled without ambiguity that any Columbia music observers who ignored Dear Blanca did so at their own peril.

Then came *I Don't Mean to Dwell.* Released last March, the record is leaner than its predecessor and marks a dramatic leap forward in emotive power and lyrical poignancy. ("Given the opportunity / I might break the old routine / Just let me know when / So I can ask off" from "Temporary Solution" remains my favorite Dickerson line. There's no metaphor, no symbolism to hunt down. That's what being in a band is like, pretty much 80% of the time, delivered as the crow flies.) *I Don't Mean to Dwell* is an exhilarating and confounding record that represented Dear Blanca at the height of what looked to be its songwriting and performative powers, its sharpest faculties firing off in one deafening burst. But apparently not content to release merely one stellar record in a year's time, Dickerson, Coty, and Powell are preparing for the September release of their fourth effort, *To Tell a Half-Truth.*

Due to the close proximity of the two records' releases and the fact that both have just five tracks each, *Half-Truth* could be considered a sort of sister record to *Dwell*, or maybe even its denouement, that gasp for the finish line in any dramatic work where loose ends are tied up, lessons are learned, and an improved social order replaces whatever clusterfuck preceded it. Where *Dwell* took earnest stabs at pop songcraft and occasionally exhibited manic, near-punk fatalism, the songs on *Half-Truth* are for the most part slower and more deliberate, willing to let the lyrics stand center-stage while compromising none of what made *Dwell*'s songs so rich.

Even by Dear Blanca standards, the lyrics on *To Tell a Half-Truth* are relentlessly melancholy. This is due in no small part to the album's credited co-writer, a poet and songwriter you've never heard of, an artist who died without a fraction of the decimal of the recognition that would appear to be his due. Countless artists leave us before their time, and this one's name was Scott Crane. He was Cameron Powell's uncle.

"My uncle – my mom's brother – passed away in the early '90s. '91, I want to say," says Powell. "Over the last twenty-five years or so our family thought we had found the grand majority of his things, and then my mom and others were cleaning out some stuff in my grandparents' attic and found a laminated presentation folder, a book – all these pages that Scott had written, so my mom told me about it. The next time I went to my grandparents' house I asked them about it and they showed it to me. It was a pretty lengthy book. There were thirty or forty songs and poems he had written and copyrighted...the majority of them were about struggling with depression and love lost, things like that. And when I told Dylan that I had this he actually had the idea of turning it into a record in and of itself."

"They're all very rooted in the heartbreak he was going through at the time," says Dickerson of Crane's unearthed works. "It doesn't feel quite like he's got his head on straight throughout the whole thing, but then in the midst of all this despair there's some really profound and poignant stuff. I tried to search for those and expand on those ideas to create a short record that represents a little snapshot of Scott's life at that time...I would look for the lines that resonated the most with me and all of those found their way pretty much verbatim onto the record."

By looking to the past to fortify the emotional power of its own present, Dear Blanca is ensuring the viability of its musical legacy, but it might also be said that the band is performing a literary service as well. The archetype of the tortured artist who perishes believing his voice will remain forever unheard is a trope as old as Kafka but, through a chance discovery, Scott Crane's words are now a matter of permanent and public record. It's almost cinematic in its narrative trajectory, a notion drummer Marc Coty confirms, albeit inadvertently. I ask him if Dear Blanca's music were to write a movie score, what kind of film would it be.

"It would have to be a drama," he answered without hesitation, "because all of Dylan's lyrics are pretty fucking sad." He pauses before adding, "I think someone would have to die in the movie."

-September, 2016

Get Out There and Kill

ANY FORM OF PUBLIC SPEAKING CAN BE A NERVE-shattering experience, but standing center stage before a roomful of strangers whose sole expectation is that you amuse them is a whole 'nother cold mug of horror as far as most people are concerned. Ask the average citizen whether they would rather undergo a thorough cavity search at the hands of an unlicensed stranger or attempt five minutes of stand-up comedy. If they don't choose stand-up immediately, they're never going to.

Based on this criteria, Jenn Snyder is not the average citizen. Hell, she might not even be the average comic. Most comedian origin stories begin with a dare at an open mic night or a tryout period wherein the would-be joke-slinger slowly realizes that the laughs just aren't coming. Jenn Snyder just wanted to skip class.

"I was thirteen and they had a talent show at my middle school," Snyder tells me over a pint at a downtown Irish pub. "Basically, the prize was that you got to miss the whole next day of class. I was going to sing because I like to sing. I told my mom about it and she was like, 'Why don't you tell jokes? You're funnier than you can sing.' So I decided to do jokes. I did jokes about my mom. I also did some prop comedy with this big pair of googly-eye glasses, you know. It was terrible but I did well enough to win and I got to do it again the next day at assembly. That's when I was like, *Yeah, this is it.*"

A wry smile creeps across Snyder's face as the memory unfolds. This is clearly a story she enjoys telling and she delivers it with the relaxed self-confidence that marks every anecdote she'll relate over the course of the afternoon. As she talks, even off the clock, it's easy to see why she's emerged over the past few years as the most popular voice in Columbia's small but passionate comedy scene. She possesses in spades something that anyone pursuing the craft should never leave home without – a genuine affinity for the spoken word. This is something all smart stand-ups understand, whether intuitively or after learning it the hard way. Even comics that employ a shy, introverted shtick – maybe especially those comics – understand that words are sneaky but powerful things. If you can't make them jibe with your specific purpose to maximum effect, then you're just up there on a stage, masturbating away while the spotlight shines.

* * * * *

Snyder's onstage persona is that of the jolly wiseass at the end of the bar, holding court for patrons and employees alike, buzzed enough to be fearless but not enough to misread the room and say something obnoxious. Her act is a time-tested blend of observational humor, wait'll-you-hear-this-shit storytelling, and raw personality. Not one to waste valuable stage time waiting for the laughs, she knows how to keep foot to pedal. If a joke doesn't elicit the intended response, she's on to the next bit, no hard feelings. Though she can be self-effacing – her weight and sexuality are both fair game and frequently mined for material –

she doesn't mind admitting that she gets what she's after more often than not, reducing entire rooms to laughter, or 'killing' in industry parlance.

On the whole, Jenn Snyder the Comedian doesn't live too far down the hall from Jenn Snyder the Person, though her Midlands-born drawl is harder to spot in the absence of a PA system. "I'm a version of myself," the Person says of the Comedian. "I'm a much more cocky, confident version of myself...I feel like I'm in that kind of Katt Williams, that kind of Eddie Murphy thing. To watch me is kind of an experience. I'm gonna move. I'm gonna be loud. I'm not just gonna stand there. You know how Steven Wright can just get up there and just deadpan deliver it? I can't do that. I'm like an animal, man. I've gotta be able to pace around and pull you in."

* * * * *

This kind of self-awareness didn't just show up in the mail one fine day, and the path from middle school clown to professional working comic wasn't a smooth one. Despite her talent show revelation, it took Snyder a while before she hunkered down and got serious. "I just dicked around in my twenties because I'm irresponsible. I just figured it would happen without me having to do any work." She hangs her head in mock embarrassment and chuckles. "That was wrong, it turns out."

Save the odd gig, this period of inaction persisted until Ma Snyder stepped in once again, sending her daughter to a weekly class in Atlanta to hone her chops so she could make an honest go of it. "I drove there once a week and took this class where they taught me, basically, how to take my thoughts and formulate them into jokes. And that's really hard. I was already conversationally funny like most people are, but this helped me come up with real jokes. I know a lot of people look down on classes like that but I thought it was awesome. Anything that helps you with your craft is not a waste of time." When I ask if she would be generous enough to divulge the formula for funny on record, her eyes roll upward as if scanning her memory drive. For the first and only time all day, she's at a loss for words. "No," she says finally. "I wouldn't know how. I don't know if it's even a real formula."

Snyder's next big move was a literal one. Four years ago, she took off for New York City in search of more opportunities. She hit every open mic she could find and took classes at New York's Comedy School where her instructor was kind enough to share some industry wisdom: She wasn't fat enough to tell fat jokes and comedy bookers don't like female comics anyway. Too wordy, she was told. She admits this shook her confidence a bit, but not for long. "It taught me something," she says of her Big Apple sojourn. "It taught me that I'm never going to quit, that this is what I'm supposed to do with my life and that fear is just one more thing you've got to overcome. And it taught me that I wasn't ready. I just went up there with a bunch of talent and I thought that would be enough. It wasn't. It wasn't enough. I needed more structure. I needed time to hone my craft."

Three months later she was out of money and back in Columbia. But brief as it was, the experience gave Snyder fresh respect for the odds she was up against and her focus narrowed accordingly. "When I came home, that's when it really happened for me," she says. "I really started to put time into these shows and cultivated comics and put in the stage time and just work, work, work. Now I feel like there's nothing I can't do."

Pressed for her overall opinion on New York, she doesn't hesitate. "I can't live in a town where people won't let you pet their dogs."

* * * * *

When Snyder says that things started happening for her upon returning home, she's not kidding. She gigs relentlessly, even taking her act as far west as Los Angeles, she's toured with infamous anti-comic Neil Hamburger, and last March she recorded her first special at West Columbia's New Brookland Tavern. The October release of *Building the Jenpire* will coincide with Snyder's next step, a move to Portland. "A really good Portland comic was telling me that when you're not from LA, you get more opportunities there because you're technically an 'out of town comic.' I'm hoping that some west coast exposure will get me where I need to be." And so Jenn Snyder will ride off into the sunset once more, bound for theoretically greener pastures, armed with jokes and scraped-knee experience.

Dog owners of Portland, consider yourselves warned.

-October, 2017

PART IV

COMMUNION PLATTERS

Dr. Roundhouse

New Society for Serious Songs

THE EXPERIENCE OF LISTENING TO DR. Roundhouse's *New Society for Serious Songs* is probably not unlike that of wandering a History of Rock museum after hours with a quartet of half-stoned curators. As musicians and songwriters, the guys in Dr. Roundhouse know the roots of and have an obvious reverence for the architects of their chosen medium, but that doesn't stop them from twisting tradition and double-knotting tropes to suit their collective personality, which happens to include a frat-house party band's taste for mischief and a hip flask's worth of wry humor. With thirteen tracks running a gamut of moods and styles, *New Society for Serious Songs* naturally has its share of misses, but these low points are by no means the rule. On the whole, the record works as a medium rare slab of guiltless entertainment with plenty of choice cuts.

"David Byrne's Funeral March" plays like a funky Talking Heads throwaway orchestrated by Frank Zappa, while "Paul's Brain" and the title track sound like Frank Z. at his most accessibly freaky. The Dr. John-inspired "Oh No, Oh Yeah!" makes a meal out of barrelhouse piano rock, "Johnny Cash" and

"What I'd Like to Know" take the piss out of hangdog Memphis country while demonstrating serious genre chops, and "I'm No Good" is the sort of jukebox rocker Lennon like to break out whenever McCartney's back was turned. "Ain't Found No Love" is *New Society*'s standout track, as well as its most relentlessly earnest. A mid-tempo slice of white-boy soul set to waltz time, the song has The Band scribbled all over it and stands as the best argument against any claim that Dr. Roundhouse has too much fun to be taken seriously.

This sort of eclecticism is usually a rookie mistake, the mark of a band so eager to please it forgoes its innate gifts in favor of that dreaded scarlet letter of mediocrity, 'Something for everyone.' But in Dr. Roundhouse's case, it's not a mistake at all, at least not a big one. The band's desire to consume and then regurgitate everything it loves about rock 'n' roll is in fact its number one strength. And on *New Society for Serious Songs*, there isn't something for everyone, but if you're the type that can hang with the weird and the wild, there just might be something for you.

-October, 2015

Glittoris

Sorry

FROM THE OPENING POWER CHORDS TO THE CLOSING wall of feedback, Glittoris has produced an album obsessed with sex on a scale capable of leaving Gene Simmons' cheeks bright rosy red. But this obsession isn't the cheesy or lascivious sort so common in rock music. Rather, *Sorry* is an angry, dagger-drawn exploration of modern attitudes toward sex and the simultaneously complex and primitive psychology that drives human desire.

Considering this record contains six tracks and barely hits the eight-minute mark, an astonishing amount of ground gets covered, ranging from lewd objectification to the non-mechanics of rough, powerhouse fucking to a detailed recounting of sexual abuse. Lead vocalist Katie Sheridan gives each subject its emotional due even when her delivery morphs from punk's patented throat-shredding into one of hyper-feminine mock innocence.

Glittoris is the sonic progeny of the Buzzcocks, the Runaways, and Black Flag. For the most part, only the latter shares Glittoris' message-is-meaning ethos, the message here being that any person who misuses others by misusing sex must be confronted with no quarter given. It's brash and unafraid, bludgeoning the listener with ideas and real-world occurrences most of us would prefer not to think about. But that's also *Sorry*'s greatest asset and the crux of its impact. "Take it or leave it," the record seems to say. "Listen or don't listen. It's no less real." The album is so unapologetic in fact that the title itself is an ironic arch-joke that only becomes apparent when the needle stops.

-October, 2015

ColorBlind

ColorBlind

THIS COLLABORATION BETWEEN SINGER AND songwriter Justin Smith and rap chieftain Fat Rat da Czar might seem strange in theory but turns out not to be a dramatic departure for either artist. In fact, the melding of their individual styles creates something singular within our fair city's musical arsenal.

ColorBlind finds Fat Rat's easygoing but insistent flow in rock-solid form while Smith remains a reliable presence on both the microphone and acoustic guitar. But, with their powers combined, they've produced a record that doesn't so much shuck the admittedly loose rules of hip-hop as pretend the rules never existed in the first place. Lead single "Live Like the Devil" is an introspective lament wherein Smith and Czar confront their respective shortcomings, brought to us with a brand of humility bereft of self-pity or put-upon kvetching. Save a lone, cavernous bass drum, light outro keys, and percussion, the instrumentation is driven by Smith's hollowed-out six-string replicating the "House of the Rising Sun" chord progression alongside a histrionic vocal delivery. Fat Rat gives the song his blessing by taking a quick verse, but it mostly feels and sounds like a Justin

Smith track that happens to feature Czar as an in-and-out guest. This makes "Live Like the Devil" something of an anomaly among *ColorBlind*'s eleven beat-driven tracks and a curious choice for a single. Despite its emotional gravitas and actual marketplace potential, it doesn't represent the project as a whole, where styles are mashed and clashed with abandon and the writing/performing workload is more or less evenly distributed between Czar and Smith.

As fate would have it, the short film announcing ColorBlind's formation was released the same day the SC House of Representatives voted to finally (*finally*) remove the Confederate Flag from the State House grounds. ColorBlind couldn't have planned this better. Nor could have the state legislature, a crew not known for its keen interest in the arts, despite inadvertently providing a perfect context for the the duo's debut. Fat Rat is black and Justin is white and their teaming-up is, in its own small way, representative of the nationwide crusade among the enlightened to demolish racial divisions and symbols thereof in ways that go beyond the ColorBlind's moniker, one of the best known cop-outs employed all too often by usually well-meaning white people who nevertheless lack the necessary empathy and the ability to think about anything consequential in the abstract.

ColorBlind's second track, "UndaGround RailRoad" embodies this spirit more than any other. It's a first-person narrative chronicling the hopes and fears of an escaped slave pursuing freedom in the North. The refrain, "I'm a runaway slave / If I was dead at least I'd be free / I'm on a runaway train / Underground railroad, set me free," is poignant enough on paper, but on the album takes on dimensions of sorrow communicable only by the human voice. It might at first seem utterly myopic that these lines are delivered by Smith and not his partner, but given ColorBlind's commitment to equality at any cost, the figurative message becomes clear: The struggle of one is the struggle of all and this can only be appreciated through honest-to-god compassion and effort. "We're all human, can't you see," Smith sings in the song's closing moments. "The inside of you is the inside of me."

-October, 2015

Jackson Spells

Jackson Spells

IN THE COMMONSENSE TRADITION, THE FIRST TRACK ON Jackson Spells' self-titled debut sets the tone and pace for all that follows. "Watching the Bats" is a haunted slice of pop paranoia, a creaky Bermuda sloop rolling atop troubled waters, delivered in a voice that burned every candle in the house at every end. Like the rest of the record, it's an exercise in the subtle, erotically-charged art of building just the right amount of tension coupled with an instinct for the perfect moment of release, even if that moment is occasionally overlooked, or just ignored.

It's tempting at this point to say something like, "Boy, these guys sure make a lot of racket for a three-piece," but that would be idiotic. A solo performer can be just as busy and loud if that's what he/she/they/it really wants. The issue isn't how much noise the trio makes but what it chooses to do with that noise, and much of *Jackson Spells* gives the impression of controlled chaos. There's a showy sense of play in the stylistic shifts of certain individual songs ("Critters"), while production contrasts between the drums and the electric piano make the two instruments sound as if they were recorded on separate planets

("Watching the Bats," "Cheap as Chum.") Sometimes, the music is content to simply self-destruct just to prove who's in charge ("Tricky Sarita.")

But for all the high-IQ hijinks, a close listen reveals a disarming sense of musical conservatism. Beneath the unhinged vocals and isosceles rhythms there's a deep reverence for the melodies and movements that have made pop music the most unkillable of unkillable beasts. It's true of course that only so much can be done with the finite number of notes in Western music and to congratulate a band for simply accepting that reality might seem intellectually lazy or vaguely fascist, but the way Jackson Spells squeezes traditional influences inside its own personality is the very engine that fuels musical progress.

Jackson Spells doesn't represent anything never-heard, yet still feels distinct, if not original. Singer John Watkins can *only* sound like John Watkins and his voice is the beating heart of the band's character. As with everything, there's filler and repetition here and there, but these quibbles don't do much to diminish the power of a record that is truly, unabashedly itself, dutifully weathering a storm of its own creation.

-October, 2015

Marshall Brown

Second Childhood

ANY NEW RECORD FROM MARSHALL BROWN FEELS like something of an event and, much to no surprise, the appropriately named *Second Childhood* was worth the wait. Within these fifteen tracks we find Brown fully embracing and actually perfecting the anything-goes Neverland pop he began tinkering with on 2013's *Through Vivaldian Colored Glasses.* Describing any music as 'Beatle-esque' runs the risk of embarrassing all parties concerned – the artist, the listener, Ringo, Yoko, etc. – but sometimes it's just the most accurate descriptor for an artful slice of pop music, so I'm using it. *Second Childhood* is the most Beatle-esque thing to appear in Columbia since Sir Paul last blew through town. It's the sound of Billy Shears diving headlong into the toybox and resurfacing to show off treasure after treasure. It's Marshall Brown being completely Marshall Brown, shameless about his influences and his ability to twist each to suit his particular needs.

The LP opens with "The Accident," a minute-thirty instrumental that sounds like Sonic Youth soundchecking with a Soft Cell B-side. This segues into "My Kite Dream," which, led by acoustic guitar and sweeping strings, evokes nothing if not

dreamlike grandeur (and kite-flying, one supposes), but by its end
has taken a jaunty turn into no-grown-ups-allowed territory, a
sentiment that will define the rest to come. "Poison Berry Jam" is
another quick instrumental set to waltz time but more ominous,
more militaristic than the opener, and then we're led into
"Dreamers at the Doors," the record's first inkling of Brown's gift
for music and vocal mimicry. In this case, he channels a young
John Lennon (which is really the only kind of John Lennon,
depending on your point of view), plaintive and haunted but
wary of succumbing to actual melancholy. "State of Grace," with
its sitar-soaked eastern psychedelia, could easily be a lost *Revolver*
cut. A fade-out brings us to "Reality Tunnel," a fifty-second
burst of British Invasion garage rock that is here and gone with
such gusto that a listener is left no time to settle into the groove.
It's a fleeting tease that plays like a movie flashback, a touchstone
we don't know yet know we're supposed to keep in our memory
bank as the record carries on. "Rare Birds" is *Second Childhood*'s
sweet tooth, a calypso-tinged slice of island pop so unrelenting in
its sunniness that one listen would send Jimmy Buffet into a crisis
of Elliot Smith proportions. "I Just Wanna Play" is the LP's most
straightforward rocker but, as its title suggests, is no more
beholden to traditional forms than anything else on *Second
Childhood*. On the penultimate track and last proper song, "I'm
So Tired," (boy loves him some Lennon) Brown really does
sound exhausted. Between the lax tempo and ever-crushing wall
of vocals, this head-to-pillow lament feels earned – not just for
Marshall Brown, but for anyone who sat shotgun with him the
whole ride through.

　　As *Second Childhood* ends, one begins to understand how
Charlie must have felt shooting out of Wonka's chocolate factory
in that great glass elevator. There's certainly something Wonka-

esque about the way Brown leads us through his second childhood, pointing out the sights and sounds, all born in a place of pure imagination. But in the end it's still only a dream. In the final track, "State of Alarm," we're treated to a snoring Marshall Brown being prodded awake by his girlfriend as the alarm clock buzzer drones on and on and on and on.... "I'm up," he says, finally.

Her curt reply: "Turn it off." And so it ends.

If this is Marshall's way of telling us that he can write some of Carolina's most masterful pop music *in his sleep*, well, message received.

-September, 2015

fk. mt.

fertilizer

FK. MT. HAS ALWAYS BEEN BETTER AT STUMBLING into punk rock than those of its peers that actively swing for it. Since the release of *underwater goddammit* in 2013, the trio has been the go-to band for charred rock dirges, and on their latest, *fertilizer*, the band hasn't made any budget cuts to their trusted artillery. Despite moments of sputtering, Isaac Brock-ish lead lines, frontman/guitarist Ryan Morris' sturdy rhythm guitar is the EP's driving force. Morris plays in lockstep with bassist Ony Ratsimbaharison and drummer Brandon Johnson (no longer a member as of this writing), giving the impression of a band that is one fat rhythm section. This lets Morris dive into the heart-on-sleeve vocal lashings that root his songs in a sort of basic, howling humanity.

In a lot of ways, Nirvana is to fk. mt. what the Pixies were to Nirvana. Kurt Cobain liked to describe his most commercially dominant song as nothing but failed Pixies rip-offs, and while *Nevermind* doesn't sound much like *Surfer Rosa* at first, second, or even tenth listen, no one ever lost brain cells tracing the lineage between those two records. Likewise, Ryan Morris can't disguise Cobain's influence on his own songwriting. But where Cobain wanted to be Frank Black and failed gloriously, fk. mt. only wants to be fk mt. *fertilizer* channels the Pixies better than Nirvana ever did and by cutting out the middleman, they've crafted a record that honors its heritage without having to answer for it. And in the often derivative realm of rock, that's an enviable brand of freedom.

-December, 2015

Autocorrect

As it Is

LIKE A HAUNTED HOUSE RENOVATED BY DERANGED orphans, Autocorrect's recorded output has been fascinating but bizarre, creepy while rewarding close exploration. The Columbia group's latest, *As it Is*, represents a turning point. Where previous albums sometimes toyed around with traditional hip-hop forms but ultimately opted to bodyboard the waves of its own innate strangeness, *As it Is* makes good on some long-held opinions that Autocorrect were always a hip-hop group at heart. And indeed, this is a legitimate hip-hop album, albeit one that plays by the band's own off-kilter rules. This is both good and bad.

The good news is that Autocorrect has finally arrived at something it had previously only hinted at and, as it turns out, really has a knack for. With bass-heavy beats and a fluid, sometimes aggressive lyrical delivery, "Overdue" and "Nomophobia" are legitimately solid tracks. If you squint hard enough, you can almost see a world where they wouldn't seem terribly out of place on mainstream radio or turning up the dance floor in some club I'll never go to. The bad news is that, for fans of Autocorrect's avant-garde tendencies, the record as a whole might skew too far toward more traditional hip-hop. At the same time, it may prove too subversive for the live-hard hip-hop crowd, bringing all of the group's latent idiosyncrasies to bear on what is otherwise a fairly straight-forward rap release.

The fourth song, "Electric" is a representative sample. After an ominous intro, the vocals run crisp and clear over a staggering beat, ripe with trip-hop fumes. The song's best lyric, "Wish in one hand / Drunk text in the other," is delivered with the tempered aggression of someone who's truly pissed off but knows he needs to blunt his anger if he expects anyone to listen. After three and a half minutes, the outro begins. Vocally, it's a high-octave send off, but it's set to a standard-issue iPhone ringtone, just one of the album's sharp left turns and one of its best moments.

Ultimately, *As it Is* works because no matter what it's doing, Autocorrect, a true original, is at its best when it brings a genre into its bubble and not the other way around. It might seem like a musical jigsaw, but it's a jumble that Autocorrect has more than figured out, assembling its varied elements with a precise, steady hand.

-January, 2016

ET Anderson

ET2

WHEN ET ANDERSON'S DEBUT *ET TU_____?* WAS dropped on us last year, it was something of a revelation. Before the record actually existed, the whole project was the stuff of gossip and whispered rumors. I recall a friend telling me in a conspiratorial tone, swearing me to secrecy, that Tyler Morris was starting a new band and it was going to blow all four walls off Columbia's rock scene while setting fire to the ceiling and the floor (I'm paraphrasing.) Morris still had plenty of goodwill left over from his previous band Calculator and great things were expected from this new endeavor. And because the universe can be sporadically benevolent to those of us who need it most, *Et Tu_____?* was indeed a stellar record. It was indie rock in the best possible sense: Indie enough to be idiosyncratic and interesting, and rocking enough to kick ass after ass in a live setting. All of the ingredients were there – lyrics clever enough to leech onto the short-term memory and vague enough to apply to anyone, guitar lines with drug abuse problems better off unchecked, and a sense of paranoia running throughout of which Fox Mulder would have doubtless approved.

And then came *ET2*.

In many ways, it's a companion piece to its predecessor. The production is consistent and the aural paranoia remains. But it would be disingenuous to treat it as though something isn't lacking. Where *Et Tu_____* felt like a complete sentence, *ET2* is a series of ellipses. I hate invoking something as cliché as the sophomore slump, but clichés usually exist for a reason. In fairness, *ET2* was largely written and recorded amidst serious personal turmoil for Morris and it would be unfair to ignore that sort of context. One would think, given the nature of his recent troubles, the resulting LP would be punk and pissed-off, waving a small army of fuck-you fingers to all those he felt had wronged him in recent months. Instead, *ET2*'s general mood is sadness and disappointment, all the way from track one to nine, if not lyrically then in overall posture. There's anger, for sure. *ET2* doesn't simply react passively. But its rage is muted, sullen, just about ready to throw in the towel.

Morris' talent as a musician and lyricist is in fine form here and deserves nothing but credit. But *ET2* sorely misses the gung-ho panache of ET Anderson's debut. But this record is by no means a failure. If anything, it succeeds as a reminder that while life can inspire and move an artist, it can also prove an insurmountable distraction.

-January, 2016

H3RO

Between the Panels

WHEN *BETWEEN THE PANELS* OPENS, WE'RE treated to one of the most truly unique spoken-word skits in the vast pantheon of hip-hop mini-dramas: Dropped into a nightmarish, post-apocalyptic world, possibly within some sort of buddy-cop context, we the listeners are bystanders in a city that is either dead or dying. Survivors are unaccounted for. It's *Mad Max* and *I am Legend*, but Mel and Will are MIA. The world is burning, just as an infamous comic book villain once wished it would. And then, interrupting the Official Motion Picture Soundtrack to certain doom, a ringing phone cuts through. It's our hero, the aptly named H3RO, calling his partner, who is nowhere to be found in this hell on earth. Whichever one is too old for this shit, let him speak now.

After a few rings, the partner answers.

"Bro, where you at?" asks H3RO, anxious.

"I don't know, man," comes the breathless response. "We must've gotten separated in the blast."

"Word. Well, we gotta try to find a way outta here somehow, man."

"Yeah. It's crazy over here."

"Keep fightin'."

"I will."

Another explosion and then the line goes dead. H3RO panics. "Light Gray? Light Gray, do you hear me?"

It's here the narrator steps in to bring us up to speed: "Another life has been lost in the Gray Area, forgotten by all but the partner he fought beside. Will he ever return? Or will he be lost for all eternity...BUT FUCK THAT SHIT! It's time to play (cue the come-on-down-next-contestant music) ... Fun and Games! With your host...ME!" It's either Bob Eubanks Mephistopheles. Right now, it doesn't matter.

H3RO has found himself the unwitting contestant of a game show that promises to be no game whatsoever. The schmaltzy music is bad enough, but then the host lays down some harsh stakes as the audience cheers like a pack of hyenas. H3RO is introduced, to frothing applause, as a comic book legend that just so happens to moonlight as – GET THIS! – a rapper! The laughter and cheers subside and H3RO is given a choice: Before him are two panels. The first will send him back to the Real World, the world of internet porn and sticky bud and disposable income where he'll get to see his family and his dog and live out a "wonderfully boring life" while leaving Light Gray behind. If H3RO chooses Panel Two, the hounds that are currently hunting and sure to kill his friend will be called off and H3RO gets to spend the rest of his life "here with ME!" But H3RO wants to go between the panels, only to be told by Dark Lord Eubanks that there's not such option.

"Fuck that," intones H3RO, taking off down the narrow path between them.

I was tempted here to just summarize the one-act opening track, but that would do a disservice to the dramatic narrative, the edge-of-death insanity, and the sheer weirdness of what H3RO clearly sees as the only way to break the seal on his record. It works marvelously as a preamble to the best nerd-rap record I've heard since I started paying Columbia taxes.

Justin Daniels (aka H3RO) is one of many young emcees currently under the tutelage of local kingpin Fat Rat da Czar. What sets Daniels apart from his contemporaries is his unabashed love for loner pastimes like comic books, video games, and good ol' masturbation. Sure, he can spout plenty of hip-hop tough-guy posturing when the spirit moves him, but he also possesses a sense of fatalistic humor and makes no effort to downplay it. "Reset (Outro)" is a prime example. How many hip-hop songs double as love letters to Playstation and the Backstreet Boys? I don't know the answer but I'm sure it's closer to zero than anything else. If H3RO is worried about street cred, it's only the street he grew up on. Besides, is there anything more dangerous than an artist actively redefining the parameters of Cool?

If not, then H3RO just might be the guy to carry the mantle of Columbia's Most Wanted.

-February, 2016

Dear Blanca

I Don't Mean to Dwell

NOT ONCE IN THE PAST THREE YEARS HAS DEAR Blanca been a disappointment. Whether on record or the stage, the band has proven that its reputation as one of Columbia's finest is hard earned and well deserved. Given this, it's not the least bit surprising that the trio's latest EP, *I Don't Mean to Dwell,* is rock-solid satisfying from the first track's opening chordal gust to the dying-battery fadeaway of the fifth.

With melancholic undertones and big choruses to part the clouds, "Joint Effort" is a fairly straightforward pop-rock song, at least by Dear Blanca standards, until the end, when the rhythmic cohesiveness is deliberately dismantled against a swing in time. As the song appears to be caving in on itself, Dickerson howls, "Goodnight, goodnight / I love you, I love you / I'll see you tomorrow" with an anguish that suggests the opposite is probably closer to the truth. "Thoughtless" is a raucous two-minute blast of beach-punk energy. The lead single, "Temporary Solution," is a breezy mid-tempo cruise-along about a near-fatal encounter between a dog and a car. It also contains the EP's best line, something familiar to anyone who's ever thrown away financial security and familial approval in the service of the slog: "Given the opportunity, I might break the old routine / Just let me know when so I can ask off." "Do You Believe Me Now" is a frantic, moody rocker with no allegiance to any single time signature, while the closer, "Ill at Ease" moves between jangly, angly verses and a rave-up chorus.

The core elements that make Dear Blanca Dear Blanca are all accounted for – the guitar lines still possess the capacity for nursery rhymes' earworm stickiness, Cameron Powell and Marc Coty still make a deceptively dynamic rhythm section, and Dylan Dickerson still sings like Gordon Gano on 60 mgs of Dexedrine. If there's a hint of something new to the proceedings, it might be because ET Anderson's Tyler Morris – certainly a kindred spirit, himself no stranger to basement rock with high emotional stakes – joins Dickerson on guitar for much of the record. *I Don't Mean to Dwell* isn't a radical departure from previous releases *Talker* and *Pobrecito*, but it just might be the band's best.

-April, 2016

Pray for Triangle Zero

Heaven & Hell

UNDER HIS AVANT-GARDE ELECTRO-POP/FREAK-rock alias Pray for Triangle Zero, Lucas Sams has released something like sixty-three records since 2009. He'll be the first to admit that it's easy to lose count. For a music critic, this sword doth have two edges. On one hand, trying to keep up with Sams' prolificness is a fool's errand. On the other, anything released in the past three months is pretty much fair game for review since he'll have something new in two weeks anyway. Blame the media all you want for society's ills. There's still a cap on how fast it can move. So let's look at *Heaven & Hell*.

Released in January, Pray for Triangle Zero's sixty-somethingth collection continues Sams' exploration of things both possible and im- within the polarizing realms of electronic and ambient music. The opening "Mess" puts its gloomy self-loathing ahead of anything like a traditional structure, but then comes "Here, Now, and There," with its jaunty, Billy Preston-ish keyboard work. "Deeper" slinks and grooves like a good fuck jam should, while "Ultimata," with its 7+ minutes running time and nods to operatic vamp-jazz, could be a GloStick-lit, digitally enhanced piano duel between Jim Steinman and Harry Connick, Jr.

With music of this sort, the line between a 'song' and a 'piece' is so thin you want to force-feed it a Jumbo Jack. 'Piece' suggests a slaved-over composition process accomplishable only by those possessing both genius and vision. By comparison, a 'song' can be written by anyone with a base understanding of structure (and maybe less) and fingers nimble enough to form three chords (and maybe fewer), created to induce pleasure or some easily identifiable emotion that isn't total panic. That's not a value judgment (I like Harry Nilsson's "Coconut" and that's literally one chord on repeat) and neither assessment is quite on the money, but I think you know what I mean. Nobody has ever said, "Boy, I just *looooove* 'Mambo no. 5!' What a terrific piece!" Outside prog, electronic, and experimental music, there's little overlap between the two. On *Heaven & Hell*, however, these admittedly arbitrary designations mingle with ease, often conflating well beyond the normal pleasure points.

-April, 2016

Boo Hag

Boo Hag

ANY TWO-MAN ROCK ENSEMBLE THAT DEPLOYS slithering riffs and oozes 'tude is going to garner comparisons to the Black Keys, so I'll get those out of the way. It's true, singer/guitarist Saul Seibert shares some lineage with Dan Auerbach – mainly his vocal delivery's effortless cool and his predilection for blues-influenced guitar lines betraying zero genre purism. Likewise, drummer Scott E. Tempo takes a big cue from Keys skinsman Patrick Carney in his studied simplicity and compulsive devotion to syncopation. The similarities pretty much end there. Boo Hag is undoubtedly its own kind of monster.

Boo Hag, from its pagan cover art to its creature-feature lyrical themes to Seibert's willingness to unleash an inhuman moon-howl whenever the spirit moves him, is a lovingly macabre document. But unlike other horror-rock acts like, say, the Misfits, whose aesthetic was complicated by one of the most self-serious frontmen in rock history, or Marilyn Manson, whose obsessive desire to become the Willy Wonka of parental nightmares turned him into little more than a human monument to cartoon grotesquerie, Boo Hag relies on neither camp nor empty shock value to draw listeners into its rock 'n' roll mausoleum. The tunes range from amped-up garage rock ("Crypt Keeper") to moody, long-haul psychedelic jams ("Buffalo"), but the whole album is united by the sense that it was recorded live in some swampy graveyard with natural, eerie reverb and insomniac spirits at the control board. Simply put, *Boo Hag* is one of the year's strongest local debuts.

-October, 2016

Sandcastles

Die Alone

IN THE THREE YEARS THAT HAVE ELAPSED SINCE
Sandcastles released *Tantrums,* there's been an obvious and
welcome musical growth. While *Tantrums* was primarily
concerned with heartache, *Die Alone* is much more of a mid-20s
coming-of-age record tackling depression, family strife, and
finding a place among one's peers. The record comes out
screaming, with Sandcastles mastermind Bakari Lebby's graveled
yelp tumbling among pointedly distorted guitars and a chorus
instructing him (us?) to "crush it 'til your chilling in your casket."
Within this roughly minute-and-a-half intro, Lebby tries to
prepare us for what's ahead, rarely holding back even *Die Alone*'s
most private emotions, inasmuch as commercially released
emotions can be considered private. Each track is an out-loud
struggle with depression, loneliness, substance abuse, and all the
misadventures that occur within the gaps.

There's an odd push-and-pull that runs through the
album. The music can be propulsive, even upbeat. Electro-tracks
like, "Okay, Cupid," "Carolina, I Love You but You're Bringing
Me Down," and "Black Sheep" are real gems. None are
overcooked and the (hopefully) litigation-ready list of samples

work together in near-harmony. "Sad Sack" is Lebby's best attempt at a straight-ahead, hook-based rock song, but it's a lyrical re-do of "Crush," and while it might inspire hope in those who need it, it's unlikely to get any anarcho-punk fists a-pumpin'. Lebby slows things down with three closing tracks that are strong and beautiful in equal measure, culminating in the title track, Lebby's finest vocal so far. It has all the symptoms of a goodbye-forever song, leaving us with a synth line that threatens an ascent into heaven, or whatever the hell is up there.

As a piece, *Die Alone* revels in melodrama, but so do we humans, imperfect as we tend to be, even at our best. Maybe you're confused or heartbroken or your favorite person has passed you by and moved someplace you'll never be able to reach them. Maybe you drink too much. Maybe you smoke too many cigarettes. Maybe there's a deadlier monkey digging its paws into your shoulder and gnawing at your earlobe. If you can see past Lebby's rampant self-absorption, you just might find your own. And that's when you'll know how truly alone you are.

-May, 2017

Say Brother

Roam

IT'S BEEN ALMOST SIX FULL YEARS SINCE COLUMBIA'S most jovial outlaws Say Brother have released anything new to the public. For a band that can claim the kind of local fanbase that these boys have earned themselves, this is no small amount of time (which, if their debut's title is to be believed, is all they got.) With only three songs, the cup hardly runneth over, but if there was any fear that Say Brother planned to hang their hats on one great record and be done with it, *Roam* is answer enough.

The EP opens with "Comfort Me," a jangly, country-tinged ode to the peace of mind that comes with knowing you've got a good woman in your corner. Carried by little more than an acoustic guitar and some melodic lead lines, "Comfort Me" isn't the sort of boot-stomper the band is known for. Still, it works as a reminder that despite their hard-earned reputation as a prison-break of a live act, Say Brother hasn't forgotten that its most important job is writing good, memorable songs. As a bonus, the track also boasts what might be frontman Tripp LaFrance's best vocal work yet as he delivers his lines with the conviction and confidence that comes with sharing the hidden parts of yourself with a willing audience.

A punk-blues rocker caked in sweat and lousy with licks, "Gimme Love" finds Say Brother in its natural habitat. The song barely cracks the three-minute mark, but if the goal is to remind a listener what this band does best, they could have pulled it off in two. Closing out the EP, the title track trades sheer hurricane force for a mid-tempo, clap-along blues groove, the result being a sort of synthesis of the preceding two songs. Most importantly, it delivers a satisfying conclusion to a record whose biggest problem is that it's too damn short.

-April, 2017

T. C. Costello

When I Was an Alien

LIKE ALL LEGITIMATE ARTISTS, GREENVILLE'S T. C. Costello has a singular vision and approach to his craft. To enter his musical world is to confront that vision, one where pop songs are almost exclusively accordion-driven, where traditional Korean music is a fair-game well to draw from, where Nirvana references can stand side by side with Zappa-esque cynicism and humor, and where party songs are self-consciously anti-party. Costello's is a world in which the anxiety of influence stands hand in hand with a truly one-of-a-kind worldview. Never has this been truer than on Costello's latest long-player, *When I Was an Alien*.

The opening title track is a fascinating exercise in intertextual interpretation. "When I was an alien," is the opening line to "Territorial Pissings," the seventh track on Nirvana's landmark *Nevermind*. That alone isn't remarkable, but consider that Costello lifts the chorus from that very song for his own, even going so far as to pinch a few lyrics. It plays more like homage than theft, given that "When I Was an Alien" isn't a rock song and doesn't pretend to be. The title could also be referencing Costello's recent time living overseas. Nirvana homage or autobiography? And for people of a certain age, what's the difference?

If you had to put a label on what Costello does, gypsy pop might be the most apt, but it still isn't quite enough. Whether he's criticizing a comrade's party prowess ("Your Partying Skills Leave Much to Be Desired") or treating a listener to an Eastern European waltz sung in what is presumably Russian ("Tumbalalaika"), Costello doesn't specialize in just one thing. He's funny, sardonic, angry and joyful, often all in one song. Still, a thirteen-track LP led almost entirely by an instrument that sounds abrasive to many Western ears may not pay the dividends he's hoping for. But given Costello's eclectic musical temperament, it would be arrogant to assume I know what he's after, if he's after anything at all.

-September, 2017

BC Villanova

Giant Light

FORMED BY SINGER/GUITARIST BRIAN CONNER, Columbia's Villanova signed with a major label in 2010 after years of rigorous gigging. It made sense. Such a band, one that hopscotched between rock, funk, and hip-hop with suspicious ease, seemed an easy fit for modern rock radio. One imagines a board room with fewer neckties than bibs, all the better for label executives drooling with abandon. But after a groaner of a name change to Weaving the Fate, chosen to avoid legal complications with a certain Philadelphia university, the suits proved reliably inept at guiding our boys through the industry trenches. The deal went away, and the band became Villanova once again.

Always seeming one lucky stroke away from hefty royalty checks and private jets, Villanova is easily Columbia's most polarizing band. If there are casual Villanova fans perched on a fence somewhere, I've yet to meet them. But the guys bother only with the positive, and that goes double for Conner, aka BC Villanova. Whether playing with Villanova, his ad-hoc backing crew, the Amazing Friends, or any of the other projects he involves himself in at will, Conner is a human round of buckshot, firing in a hail of separate directions at a common target. Now with *Giant Light*, he can pad out his CV with an official solo record. The album only strengthens the case that if the universe were slightly different, Conner would be a legitimate mainstream force, soul patch and all.

There's a lot about *Giant Light* that merits a double-take. There's the fact that the rest of Villanova will back up BC when he performs this solo material, for example. Or that he sounds straight-up peppy during lyrically dour ballads. Or his hot idea to close the record with nearly six minutes of spoken-word "Thank Yous," which takes a scythe to any musical momentum that might have ended the record. But the bright spots make *Giant Light* worthwhile and they're easy to find. "Dark Days" rocks surprisingly, almost alarmingly hard, while "Good Day" evokes *Songs About Jane*-era Maroon 5, the modern prototype for wasted potential. Still, the album is by no means a start-to-finish triumph. Songs like "Get Hurt" and "Hard to Be Around" are pure vanilla extract, equally capable of FM glory as being forgotten entirely.

Giant Light finds Conner still following the same artistic inclinations he always has, which means gearing himself toward the widest possible audience. Never one to pander, Brian Conner is ridiculously gifted at making the mainstream push seem downright charming, which isn't a small thing. If music's potential to appeal to a gargantuan swath of strangers strikes you as the province of cowards, go dig up some Belle and Sebastian. I'm just thankful some people still want to be rock stars.

-November, 2018

PART V

CONFESSIONS FOR THE ROAD

Stoned Puppies Forever

FRANK CAME DOWNSTAIRS INTO THE LIVING ROOM where, in the bookshelf corner, Lilith was bloodying the last unclaimed blanket in the house. Margot and Scott were on the sofa watching her. "If you guys want to say your goodbyes, this is the time to do it," he said.

"I don't know if I can handle that right now," said Scott.

"There isn't much choice."

"How is she?"

"Confused. Practically dead."

Scott wiped his cheeks and forehead. "Do I look normal?"

"For you, I guess," Frank said, and kneeled beside Lilith. She was panting gusts but otherwise hadn't made much noise since the whole thing started. "I wonder how many she's going to have."

Margot turned to the TV news where a man in a suit was pretending to know the next day's weather. Scott inspected his pupils in the mirror by the front door and then climbed the stairs until his footsteps disappeared somewhere overhead. There were three little ones so far – spotted, blind, all squirming and soft cries.

"What are you going to say to Gram?" asked Frank.

"I don't know, but it'll be kind of hard getting up those stairs with a busted foot, don't you think?" Margot kept her focus on the TV screen as she said this.

"I'll help you."

She almost faked a laugh. "Whatever you say."

"Oh, just let it go," he said. "I already told you I was sorry." He scratched Lilith's ear and she looked up at him in gratitude.

"You sure did. Like always."

"Didn't Scott give you one of his pain pills?"

"Yeah."

"Did you take it?"

"I gave it to her," she said, jerking her head toward the corner.

"To Lilith? When?"

"While you were upstairs. I figured she needed it more than me."

"What's the matter with you? You know Scott takes those really strong ones." He stared at her but the TV had her full attention. "Jesus," he said, walking into the kitchen. "It's gonna be in her milk now, you know." He came back with a bowl of tapwater and placed it next to Lilith's blanket, but she was distracted by another one sliding out, breathless.

* * * * *

Though he had sat and played on its nog-yellow carpet more times than he knew, Scott came to the windowless bedroom at the hallway's end with an explorer's anticipation of the unfamiliar. He tapped his fingertips on the open door. "Gram? You awake?"

There was no response and the room was too poorly lighted to make out more than the mere suggestion of a figure in the bed against the wall. He went in and stood over her. The air was stale and heavy and the lamp on the bedside table poured a modest trickle of light across her rosary and the scattered inhalers and medicine bottles. The ceiling fixture had burned out years ago. By that time, he and Frank and Margot had long since abandoned the bedroom as a hideaway from all of the things outside its four walls that seemed so deliberately mundane and unfair. As it always had, the walk-in closet in the corner stood open, but instead of Grandpa Dick's museum of overcoats and the constant litter of dolls, trucks, and picture books on the shelves and floor, there were only a few lonely coat hangers. The big wooden desk was gone. Scott wasn't sure if he'd ever noticed before now. Gram had always called it the work desk, though he couldn't remember anyone ever using it for work. Instead, he and his cousins would huddle underneath among its ancient oak legs and pretend there was a search party out for them, like they were special people worth recovering. Sometimes in the dark they would take Grandpa Dick's flashlight with them and Scott would read out loud from the ghost story book they kept in the top drawer. Margot would get scared and beg Frank, often through tears, to take her to their mother. Sometimes he was able to calm her down and sometimes she was made to simply suffer through. Still, she never left his side.

The bed had been theirs, too. Whenever staying overnight, they splayed between the sheets like a threepile of runts, always with a threadbare view of the nightlight keeping vigil in the hall. And now here she was. Under the covers, lacy gray nightgown matted up under her chin, lids fluttering, attended only by hanging photographs of everyone she had accidentally outlived.

"Gram?"

She turned toward his voice. "Richard?" The word dragged from her mouth like a wisp of smoke.

"No, it's me, Scott."

She moved to raise herself and then, finding it impossible, settled slowly back down. "Richard, what are you doing home at this hour?"

"No, Gram. It's Scott."

She studied his face through stormcloud eyes. "Scotty?"

"Hey, Gram."

"What time is it?"

"It's a little after seven."

"Is your grandfather home yet?"

Scott shook his head. "No, Gram. He isn't here."

"I swear, if he's been out –" she began, but then lurched into a violent coughing fit. Scott thought he heard the blood and fluid boiling over and crashing against her lungs like tiny waves. He sat on the edge of the bed and waited while she hacked and struggled to reclaim air. Composed for the moment, she looked to the doorway and then back. "Your cousin was just in here visiting." Her voice was small and distant and she punctuated her sentences with a deep swallow as every breath became increasingly precious and unnecessary.

"Yeah. He's back downstairs with Margot."

"Margot? Did she come for supper, too?"

"She did. How are you feeling?"

"She's turned out to be such a beautiful young woman. I always knew she would."

He nodded and began to count her medicine bottles, only to realize he already knew there were eleven.

"She gets those long eyelashes from her mother."

"How are you feeling, Gram?"

"And her mother got them from me, you know."

"I know."

"Is Margot staying for supper?"

"Yes, Gram," Scott didn't know if he should be crying but decided he might try later.

She started to say something else but the words cracked and fell to dust as breath escaped her again. Her chest heaved under the blanket, slowly at first and then rapidly. He took her hand, trying not to squeeze too hard. Her lungs released all they had left to reckon with.

* * * * *

"What's the matter with it?" asked Margot, limping across the floor to the corner.

Frank was hunched on his heels over Lilith's fourth. "It isn't breathing."

"It was fine a second ago, right?"

"I thought so. But it won't move."

Side by side, they hovered over the tiny thing, Frank poking its hairless belly and Margot watching, careful to keep her weight off the bad foot. Its eyes were closed like its sisters' and brothers', but where they were busy blindly scouting for their mother's underside, this one lay alone, untrembling and without a sound.

Scott appeared at the bottom of the stairs. "What's going on?" he asked, and came over to see.

"Doesn't look like this one's gonna make it," said Margot.

Lazy-eyed but careful not to disturb the others, Lilith adjusted herself and lowered her head beside it. She breathed it in and licked its back, then prodded it with her nose. It didn't move and never would.

Scott leaned in closer. "Aw, shit. What happened?"

"I can take a guess," said Frank, the words dangling just beneath his breath.

Margot glared. "You don't know what happened. This kind of thing happens all the time."

"What do we do with it?" asked Scott. "We can't just throw it away."

"We'll bury it in the morning."

"Do you think she's gonna have any more?"

Lilith rolled her eyes up at them as if curious herself.

"Doubtful," said Frank. "She's spent."

Scott helped Margot to her feet and supported her as they all moved to the back patio for cigarettes in the frosted air.

Lilith stayed behind, exhausted and weak, stretched out while the newborns drained her for all they could get. They could not have known it, but they were happier now than they would ever be, no matter how long they lived.

Homebody

THE MAN DID NOT BELIEVE IN GOD. HE NEVER HAD, not even when he was young and others would threaten him with tales of endless fire if he didn't change his mind. But the way the water was coming down – ceaseless and aggressive and without shame – he couldn't help but imagine that it was the doing of some otherworldly authority. Being a man of neither religion nor science, he burned through each theory with ease until there were none left. It hadn't stopped raining for days – morning, afternoon, evening, or nighttime.

He had a job in an office several blocks away from his home, no car, and had somehow never acquired an umbrella, so on the first day he walked to work and then home from work in the hot, heavy rain that came down like precious stones upon his head and shoulders and putrefied everything in his world. It had started in the morning and continued long after he'd gotten home and cooked dinner. It continued as he sat in front of his television and ate and then while he was lying in the darkness in bed, staring up at a ceiling he couldn't see, listening to it pound against the roof and his bedroom window, demanding entry. It was still raining when he woke up on the morning of the second day. Again he walked to work and then home from work in the rain, arriving at each place with his hair and shirt and tie and pants soaked to their limpest, most basic pulp and his black shoes squeaking with every step in any direction.

It rained from time to time in the city where he lived, as in all cities, but never like this. It never broke, never slackened in its resolve. The third and fourth days proceeded as had the first and second. He was either wet or recovering from wetness at all times. Never fully dry or comfortable. On the fifth day he awoke in his bed and decided to stay there, listening. He listened to the water pummel his shelter and attempt to breach it. After an hour or so the phone rang. It was the man's boss. The boss asked him where he was and why he hadn't come to the office. He told his boss that he was sick and would not be coming in today and the boss asked why he hadn't called beforehand to let someone know. The man told him that he was too sick to call but thanked his boss for checking up on him. The boss asked the man if he was going to come into the office tomorrow and the man said yes, he probably would. Then he got back into bed and spent the rest of the day listening, getting up only to eat, twice.

The next morning, he was in his kitchen washing dishes. Again he hadn't gone to the office. The phone rang. He knew it was his boss and didn't answer. He didn't feel like explaining to the boss that he had decided not to leave home until the whole thing stopped. He knew his boss wouldn't understand. The phone rang several more times throughout the morning and afternoon but he left it alone. He only napped and watched television and took regular meals. Still the rain didn't stop. In fact, it only seemed to be falling and churning upon the city with greater zeal.

* * * * *

Now it had been raining for one week. The man was preparing lunch when the phone rang. Out of guilt, he answered. It wasn't his boss as he had expected, but his mother. She said that the boss had called her and asked if she had heard from the man, that he had not been coming to work in the office. She asked him why he had not been going to work and he told her he wouldn't be going anywhere until the weather changed. She didn't ask why because she didn't care why. She told him to stop being a fool and go back to work. The man promised his mother that he would return to the office the next day and said goodbye. While eating his lunch the man realized that the food in his home was dwindling in supply and he would soon have to venture out for more, but knew he couldn't. He was dry now and had been for two days because he'd stopped showering. To shower would mean feeling hard water shooting down and over every naked inch and he couldn't bear the thought. He drank, but that was all.

The rain continued and by the ninth day he had eaten all he had to eat. The phone had been ringing for days. He spent the tenth day in bed with his hands over his stomach, listening to the rain bellow and the phone scream, hating both and wishing they would go away. He got out of bed on the eleventh day and answered the phone, sick of its incessant yawl, expecting his mother or his boss, but the voice on the other end was one he didn't recognize, of indeterminate sex, speaking a language that troubled him. "Who is this," he asked. "What is all this about?" But he received no discernable answer. Words were spoken, he knew that much, but he couldn't attach any meaning or ideas to them. They began calmly but increased in intensity until the receiver began to burn to his ears. He slammed it down and then collapsed onto the kitchen floor.

He eventually came to but didn't know how long he had been lying there. He heard the rain and the wind outside, howling on. He was in terrible pain from hunger and dehydration and poured a glass of water from the sink. He drank it down and then had another. The mere thought of water touching him anywhere, even just his lips and the inside of his throat as it went down made the man feel more ill. He knew he needed the water or else he would die, and he was afraid to die as men often are, but his fear of a slow, isolated death didn't supersede his desire to never feel the rain again upon his skin as long as he lived, even if that wasn't long at all. He went into the living room and stood, looking at nothing but the shuttered window with thick curtains drawn tight. He didn't see much light from the other side anymore, only dark blue clouds and the screaming rain. He collapsed again just as the phone began ringing again. This time he didn't hear it.

* * * * *

The man was suddenly conscious and realized he didn't know what day it was. He didn't care, he just didn't know. He only knew he was going to die and felt a modicum of surprise every time he woke up. Whether the bed or the bedroom floor or the kitchen floor or the couch in the living room, he didn't understand why he was still alive and then began to question whether he really was. How long could it last? He was naked all the time because the stench of his own flesh disgusted him, but that disgust reminded him that he was still capable of revulsion and he came to savor it. He was crippled with hunger. Every now and then the phone would ring and he thought sometimes that he might answer it but had neither the strength nor the courage. Flies would rest upon his arms and face and sometimes he swatted them off.

* * * * *

One day or possibly one night there was a knock at his front door. It startled him out of a heavy fugue and he kept his hands to the wall as he staggered to the door. Here he is, the man thought. He is here finally to take me. The knocking continued and as the man approached the door a voice came through, hollow against the rain. "Hello, hello? Are you in there?" The man recognized the voice. It was his boss's assistant, a short and usually nervous man. He continued to shuffle towards the door and tried to respond but his throat was coated in lead and dust and he only managed the faintest cry, less a spoken word than the whisper of a beaten ghost. He dropped to the floor, balancing on his heels like a defecating dog. "I can hear you," the assistant said through the door. "Don't pretend you aren't in. I hear you moving around in there." The doorknob turned but the door was locked, which the man didn't remember doing. "It's me," said the assistant. "Let me in.'

The man coughed up rust before finally managing, "What do you want?"

"Open the door."

"I can't."

"Why not? Are you hurt? You won't answer your phone and the boss wanted me to come and see if you were okay or even still alive. Open up."

"Go away."

The assistant's voice struck higher now to cut through the thousands of angry fists begging to be let in as well. "What's happened in there? Are you coming back to the office?"

"Not until the rain stops."

"What did you say?"

"Not until it stops."

"It sounds like you might need some help. Open up and let me in."

"Leave me alone."

"Alright, but you should know that it's never going to stop. This is how it is and if you aren't back in the office tomorrow you can consider yourself unemployed. Do you understand what I'm telling you?"

The man said nothing and after a few moments he heard shoes clap away through the water. He fell from his heels and stayed curled up like a skinless baby in front of the door for the rest of whatever it was. An hour. Two days. He didn't know.

* * * * *

He was too skinny now. Too skinny to be alive, he thought whenever he looked down at himself and saw his ribs protruding through his stomach, which had gone sickly pale. His entire body looked dusted with chalk – not pale, but empty of color and he wondered if perhaps he was becoming an egg. He smelled himself all the time. Rotting meat and copper. He could no longer walk. When he felt it was time to move, he crawled from room to room, usually with his legs stretched out behind him as he lay belly-down and used his hands or elbows to drag himself along. Most of the time he would simply wake up in one room or another, often without any memory of how or why he came to be there. At one point there was once another knock at his front door, but whoever was on the other side never tried to get in or call to him. There were insects all over his house. Roaches scuttled across the floor and flies thrummed together in little black clouds around his head. None of them were afraid of the man.

* * * * *

Another day – he couldn't be sure when – there came another knock at the door and he almost died of fright from the sound. The knocker knocked more and then yelled through the door, warning him about the limits of his power. This was interrupted when the phone rang. He needed help and decided to answer it. He could barely speak, instead only utter exhaust but, after some false starts, he said, "Hello, it's me."

On the other end was the same voice from long ago, muttering curses in the same indecipherable tongue. Nothing he knew or could make sense of.

"It's me," the man said as best he could, talking over the voice. "Please tell me when this is going to stop."

The voice on the other end carried on, intoning darkly without pause.

"I know, the man said, trying to conceal the fear in his voice. "I should have decayed a long time ago."

At this, the voice stopped, but only or a moment, and then burst into peels of laughter and the line went dead.

* * * * *

The man woke up some time later on the living room couch. The throw pillow was coated with flecks of dead skin and spongy with sweat. There was an audible thickness in the air, some static belch that filled the room. It was stifling dark all through his home. He heard the faint tapping of something distant or small upon the floor and wondered if it was a cockroach sending out Morse code. He slid off the couch and put his ear to the floor and listened, but couldn't make anything out or understand its phrases. "I know you're trying to help me but I don't understand," he tried to say, but the words disintegrated.

The messenger crawled upon his cheek and waited to be swooshed away, but it never happened. Feeling brave, it brushed its antennae through dirty whiskers and climbed into an open mouth where it felt so at home in the airless warmth that it settled there for the rest of its life.

Click Goodbye

CAREFUL AS HE COULD BE NOT TO WAKE HIS sleeping daughter, he tiptoed as if on padded rabbit feet over her bedroom's fine white carpeting toward the window. There were toys on the floor, never laid out the same or else he would have memorized them by now, and the waxy strip of moonlight that fell through the curtain and onto the floor was barely enough to keep him from stepping on a squeaky one or cutting a toe on something sharp down there. He had reminded his sleeping daughter numerous times when she was awake that big girls clean up toys when they're done playing with them, and didn't she want to be a big girl too? She always said yes, she did want to be a big girl, but she kept forgetting how, as little girls always do.

In his white undershirt and brown flannel sleep pants, he made it to the window. The curtain was of thick material and hung over his back like a cape as he hunched low enough to raise the window. He eased it up slowly, pausing to note any disruption in his sleeping daughter's wispy breathing, but there was none. She slept well for someone so young. Rare was the night that she suffered an unpleasant dream and was forced, by her own mind's power to frighten her, to crawl into bed with him and his sleeping wife and nestle between them so closely that either could have rolled a wrong turn and crushed her in the night.

She'll be doing this too one day, he thought, climbing up and out. Probably believing she herself the first to do it, she'll creep out and likewise stand on the edge, or safely near it, and take in the raw pleasure of a virgin night. No sun to expose you to the world below, only a weighted quiet you forgot existed against the lowering backdrop of the morning and its music. Distant tires humming in this or that direction, cracked leaves swooshing past one another in a race with no discernible finish line, and the birds. Everyone hated the birds it seemed. Others would speak of them with such frustration, as if the bane of their lives could be found every morning just before the first natural light, in the trees outside every window of every bedroom in every house in every part of the world. And they were only singing. He didn't hate them and wondered if she, who was behind him now, still sleeping inside, would hate them when her time came to climb out here, believing she was the first.

The birds had started without him but grew excited as they spied him from the naked branches. This morning's selection was a call-and-response number, with this little guy over here whistling away a few bars only until he stopped and his contemporary far back that way picked it up, adding variations to their established themes. He breathed deeply as they welcomed him. The shingles below his long-calloused feet were sturdy but he still moved slowly, just as he had in his sleeping daughter's bedroom. The roof spread out in either direction, giving view to the torsos of taller trees and neighboring houses and their unoccupied roofs. The moon was low and fading and saying faretheewell, but by its dim radiance and a bare thread of memory, he knew there was a house like his on the opposite side of the street, as there had always been, even when he was a boy living in a different one with a different roof and little signals speaking to him from just ahead, cutting through the dark.

* * * * *

His parents had no problem with him owning his own flashlight, precious and important tool that it was. "Just don't stay up too late reading," his father had warned when they returned from the store and the flashlight, having already passed inspection, was cradled under his arm. In the kitchen making dinner, his mother offered similar advice, believing that a boy who spent his nights reading under tented bedsheets would be of no use the following day at school.

At bedtime he practiced. One click on and off to announce your presence. Another longer wink of light to say Hello. Goodnight the same. What existed in between was a language largely made of thrown silences careening over a distance nearly immeasurable in the spilled ink of night. He practiced, timing the flashlight and himself, rehearsing and remembering and nervous that he might shoot her too long or short a beam, accidentally communicating a message neither would understand. He couldn't sleep that night, not before and certainly not after Cora came into his window as she had been doing, teasing and searching and saying Wake up with her bobbing ball of light breaking through his curtain and onto his bare feet hanging just at the edge of the bed. The light vanished when he opened his window and climbed out. She had cleared her throat and said hello but now he could do the same. Flashlight in hand and one short click to announce himself, a bit longer then to say Hello, I see you, you are far away, but we are the same.

At school, Cora had friends and he had friends, but they were not the same friends. She sat in the first row of science class every day, although being neighbors at home and in science class is not always reason enough to speak. By the time the first light on the first night shone through his curtain, he had formed a relationship with the back of her head. From one row behind and two seats to the left he had come to know her ears and their elfin peaks, but only saw them when her brown-red hair was up, tucked and woven neatly through an elastic tie. Her voice was sweet and showed little trace of the fear children battle when called upon to answer the question their teacher is asking them. She didn't even seem embarrassed when she was sometimes wrong.

He had stumbled out onto the roof on that first night after waking in a panic at the light swirling over his walls and floor and dresser drawers, thinking it must be a broken streetlight or collapsing moon, and then looked out just in time to see it disappear. She had tortured him by shining it from her perch outside her own window directly into his eyes. He shielded them, still confused, until she roped it back and lit her own face. Down and messy, her hair fell like drapes and lent her eyes a symmetry he would never have noticed up close. Then one short click goodbye and she crawled back through her own window, leaving him to scuttle back through his. Cora had said hello.

He dreamed all through the next day's science class that Cora would turn around and meet his eyes but she never did. That night, however, to his terror and joy, she was back. Sitting Indian-style on the roof outside her bedroom in her lacy white nightgown, raygunning him while the whole world slept, she wordlessly demanded that he stand at attention in his embarrassing footie pajamas and allow himself to be probed, illuminated and explored. She ran her light slowly up his leg and then hovered there at his waist before letting it glide down the other. Descending further, the orb began to shake belligerently at the tips of his footied toes before dancing its way back to the edge. One short click goodbye.

It wasn't until four nights later, after being spotlighted and examined by Cora and her flashlight, that he had one of his own and could now be an active partner in the curious dance that was gaining steam. He hunkered down with a woolen blanket draped over his neck and she would sometimes stand and float from one dark edge of her parents' roof to the other, but mostly crossed her legs and leaned forward into his light to be better seen.

It was on the seventh night of his and Cora's blinding one another with their flashlights that she removed the nightgown. Placing a hand to its opposite shoulder, she slid the thin straps aside until they hung at her elbows before giving in and the whole of the sleeping dress collapsed exhausted around her ankles. She did not at any point step out of the mesh puddle at her feet. She didn't move at all. She simply stood and turned off her light, while his raked the trees and shot off infinitely into the night sky, so when he returned to her to ask, through the evolving cadence of their nuanced language, where she had gone, the answer was right there in front of him. I have not gone anywhere, she said. I am here, more here and more present than I have ever been before.

His heart hurt and then froze. Not out of fear, but something he had never felt and therefore couldn't name. As she stood out there on the roof across the street wearing nothing but his light, he didn't feel any of the things he thought he would feel when he finally saw what he was finally seeing. He thought that he would barrel through any obstacle, slay sea monsters and bound across rooftops just to touch her. Instead, he felt grateful and ashamed. He was grateful that she was strong and brave and trusted their language so fiercely that she could cross whatever rickety bridge separates the soul of a child from that of an adult. He was ashamed because he wasn't.

Her hair was pillow-wrecked, her chest was as flat and bony as his, and her hips showed no interest in protruding in any direction except straight down, streamlining the path from breast to knee his hands might have taken had he been physically closer and less knotted up inside. The white dress hanging lazily over her feet made it impossible to tell if her toenails were painted, but he knew (or thought he knew) that they were. Small, shiny red or purple tufts over each toe, descending in size. Her knees bent in to greet one another and her arms hung at her sides. He was thankful she couldn't see his face. And then, as he was preparing to invent new words with his fingers on the on/off button, she collected the little dress from her feet and disappeared. Without a wave, a smile, or a soft mashing of her lips, she vanished back into her bedroom through the curtain. It was then that the birds began singing. They were soft at first, testing the acoustics, and then grew confident and sang a song so spirited and all-at-once peaceful that he lost his footing for a moment, thinking himself the object of mockery. But he gathered himself and sat down, listening to them. He wasn't ready for bed. He wasn't ready for a song either but, unlike the bed, the song crawled sleepily into him.

Science class the next day had an empty seat in the first row. He felt, with guilt, a sense of relief. After all, how does one sit stare at the back of another person's head, knowing that the person is

more than a person – a phantom in fact, or a signal in a vacant
sky telling you that you're needed and wanted. She was likewise
absent on the roof that night. He sat with his flashlight on and
the beam straddling the spaces around his feet so that, if she
came out or peered through the glass and white curtain, she
would see him and know she hadn't made a mistake. But Cora
never showed. When the birds began to sing he gave one short
click goodbye and retreated inside.

She was absent again the next day and night from school
and the roof, and then again the next. When the gray-haired
science teacher called roll each morning, her name was skipped,
like she'd never been there at all. No one spoke of her and the
girls she typically walked the halls and ate her lunch with
appeared to be carrying on perfectly fine without her. It made
him feel forgotten, too.

It was over dinner on the third day of Cora's absence that
his mother said to his father, while chewing a forkload of mashed
potatoes, "And did you hear about Glen? He's real sick."

"I know, poor guy," his father said. "But that's what
smoking will do to you."

"Beth next door talked to April, and there's a doctor out in
Arizona they're gonna try."

"Well, I don't know about all that, but they'd better get
out there soon if they're at least gonna give it a shot."

"Oh, they've already left. Took their little girl out of school
and everything."

He muscled down his meal and his mother and father
moved on to the weather.

There was an image of her that lived in his memory. The way her hair fell, its natural inclination to wrap somehow under her chin, those pointed ears and the distance between her eyes. But under a night sky so bloody and bluish and with so many gaseous specks burning themselves to rubble above, with his light the only trusted eye and the pitch black landscape of their separate young lives melting away around her into the ether, no vision could have been seen more clearly by any man anywhere, of any age.

* * * * *

And now, standing on the shingles of a roof in a house different in size and city and basic structure from the one he had lived in as a boy, he trod softly around as not to wake his sleeping daughter and to experience the song from all possible aural vantage points. The birds singing in the East sang differently from those on the Western side and, although they functioned nicely as a whole, he could never quite predict when one would catch the spirit and take off, whistling high and proud above his fellows, even for a second. He listened and softly kicked at the brown and yellow leaves that were collecting around the gutters and when the moon had completely passed, allowing the early morning sun to peer over the horizon, he moved the thick curtain of his sleeping daughter's bedroom window aside and ducked back in. His sleeping wife would soon be awake and there was coffee to brew in the kitchen. And once they'd drank a cup and talked about how yesterday went and what today might be like, his wife would go back upstairs and wake their sleeping daughter for school while he tucked in a clean shirt and tied a tie underneath his collar.

He loved his sleeping wife and took pride in their give-and-take approach to raising their sleeping daughter. He bought her birthday presents and his wife decorated the bedroom. He decided when the television went off and she decorated the girl's hair. He named this child and she would name the next. Back when his wife told him she was pregnant with a little girl, she suggested a Biblical name, something that would be hard for mean kids to make fun of. But he had another name for her. It was a name he loved to say aloud in private moments while the birds sang and he wanted a reason to say it in front of others so that maybe, by some small chance, they could hear the music in it and feel the calming peace of a name so short and pretty it could only belong to a little girl, sleeping or not.

AFTERWORD

EVERYTHING IN THIS BOOK WAS WRITTEN BETWEEN 2008 and 2019, roughly the decade I lived and worked in Columbia, South Carolina after graduation. During this time, I waited tables and tended bar to keep the lights on as I pursued my dream of drumming for the most hard-rockin' band in this world or any other. I'd be lying if I said I remembered exactly when, but one night, somewhere along the way, I was darkening a booth at Art Bar when I happened upon fellow townie Pat Wall. Back then, Pat was the music editor for Columbia's *Free Times*. He made a living from not just writing, but writing about *music,* which meant he was, at least in my eyes, a man not to be trifled with. Nevertheless, the scene I'm presented with whenever I think back on that evening is one in which I've got Pat pretty well cornered near the main bar and am hovering over him in a way that would lead any reasonable person to assume I'd given up on social norms. He's rendered in full color and dressed in normal, period-appropriate street clothes, while I'm a lurching, shadowy figure wearing what is

either a pea coat or a cape and whose limbs bend in ways those
of a righteous man simply do not. Somehow failing to notice his
eyes darting around the room as he searches for an escape plan, I
keep a bourbon steady with one hand and artlessly jam a finger
in his face with the other. By pretty much any standard, I am
trifling with him.

Whenever I re-experience this interaction, I do so not as a
participant but as an onlooker. This could offer a unique
perspective in many cases, but in this one I'm seated too far from
the action to hear the actual dialogue so it's just a lot of me
scowling and pointing and clutching my glass and him nodding
and sweating and smiling until he's eventually able to pry himself
away, at which point the scene collapses into static until
something new starts up, not unlike a VHS home movie.

Obviously, my long-term memory has taken some liberties
with the details and I assume (hope, really) Pat recalls the
encounter differently. In any event, whether I threatened and
intimidated a local journalist into giving me a job (this strikes me
as unlikely) or just asked him if there was room for one more on
the freelance staff (much more in keeping with my negotiation
tactics before and since), the takeaway is the same. I sent Pat a
few writing samples the next day and before either of us had the
chance to change our minds, my first byline appeared in *Free
Times,* where it could be reliably found every week for the next
several years. That first gig led to a second, which led to another
and another and so on until what might have started as a hobby
or a way to earn a little extra money (I don't remember what role
I assigned it back then, honestly) has gradually become a means
to an invaluable end – sharing a few thoughts on something that
gives life its vitality with anyone who cares to read them and, in
doing so, sharing so much of myself.

And that brings us to *Surf's Up in Purgatory*.

There's no valid reason for this book to exist other than my belief that it should. If that strikes you as self-indulgent, I suppose I can understand why. But that's not how I see it. The way I see it, a formative chapter in my personal and professional life has come to a close and no matter where I go or what I do from here, I'll have a permanent record – not just of my own work during that rough decade, but of a city whose musicians and artists are finally beginning to get some of the non-Hootie recognition they deserve.

Speaking of recognition, I owe a debt of gratitude to the following people, without whom this book would be significantly worse or altogether unrealized: Greg Slattery, David Travis Bland, Kyle Peterson, James D. McCallister, Patrick Wall, Jordan Lawrence, Heyward Sims, Eva Moore, Cindi Boiter, Michael Rouse, Jeremy Ray, Scott West, Web Hulon, the Eagles Fastlane fan club, Brett Kent, Josh Bumgarner, George Fish, Andy Auvil, Ameer Raja, Julian C. Scott, the Spawn clan, and Mary Miles.

SURF'S UP IN PURGATORY

63062717R00117

Made in the USA
Columbia, SC
08 July 2019